Praise for *In*

"I am completely floored by this book. What Sadiya Ansari manages to accomplish here is a rare, miraculous feat—a high-wire act of boundless empathy and incisive investigation. *In Exile* is a curious and profound book, as rigorous as it is tender. When a writer is willing to be this honest and this vulnerable, it is always a gift that I do not take for granted. Sadiya carefully pulls together threads of painful family history and questions that go unspoken to create a deeply poignant and unforgettable work."
—Elamin Abdelmahmoud, author of *Son of Elsewhere: A Memoir in Pieces*

"*In Exile* is a study in making choices that reverberate across generations. It adds an important vantage point to the aftermath of the Partition and how it continues to shape so many. It's a rallying cry to honour our pasts. Sadiya's journalistic eye offers a crucial historical glimpse into what was lost during the Partition."
—Samra Habib, author of *We Have Always Been Here: A Queer Muslim Memoir*

"*In Exile* is more than a memoir, it's a fascinating excavation of Sadiya Ansari's family mythology. Devastating, sensitive, and generous, *In Exile* is a beautiful story of how women caught in the middle of politics and patriarchy make the hardest of decisions. A searing, gorgeous read."
—Jen Sookfong Lee, author of *Superfan: How Pop Culture Broke My Heart*

"*In Exile* blends the best of memoir, mystery, and investigative journalism. Wry and relatable, Sadiya Ansari is a gifted storyteller who confronts the impacts of Partition and the pitfalls of memory to piece together a personal history that poses broader questions about what it means to be a wife, a mother, and a woman—and what happens when women take meaning into their own hands. Filled with vulnerability and revelation, this book explores what unexpected flowers may bloom from even the most tangled family roots."

—Anuja Varghese, author of the Governor General's Literary Award–winning *Chrysalis*

IN EXILE

RUPTURE, REUNION,

AND MY GRANDMOTHER'S

SECRET LIFE

SADIYA ANSARI

ANANSI

Published in Canada in 2024 and the USA in 2024 by House of Anansi Press Inc.
houseofanansi.com

House of Anansi Press is committed to protecting our natural environment. This book is made of material from well-managed FSC®-certified forests, recycled materials, and other controlled sources.

House of Anansi Press is a Global Certified Accessible™ (GCA by Benetech) publisher. The ebook version of this book meets stringent accessibility standards and is available to readers with print disabilities.

28 27 26 25 24   2 3 4 5 6

Library and Archives Canada Cataloguing in Publication

Title: In exile : rupture, reunion, and my grandmother's secret life / Sadiya Ansari.
Names: Ansari, Sadiya, author.
Description: Includes bibliographical references.
Identifiers: Canadiana (print) 20240328507 | Canadiana (ebook) 20240328671 |
ISBN 9781487012373 (softcover) | ISBN 9781487012380 (EPUB)
Subjects: LCSH: Ansari, Sadiya—Family. | LCSH: Women—India—Punjab—Social conditions—
20th century. | LCSH: Family secrets. | LCGFT: Biographies.
Classification: LCC HQ1744.P86 A57 2024 | DDC 305.40954/552—dc23

Cover design: Andreea Muscurel

House of Anansi Press is grateful for the privilege to work on and create from the Traditional Territory of many Nations, including the Anishinabeg, the Wendat, and the Haudenosaunee, as well as the Treaty Lands of the Mississaugas of the Credit.

 Canada Council for the Arts   Conseil des Arts du Canada   ONTARIO ARTS COUNCIL / CONSEIL DES ARTS DE L'ONTARIO an Ontario government agency / un organisme du gouvernement de l'Ontario

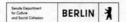 With the participation of the Government of Canada / Avec la participation du gouvernement du Canada   Canadä

Senate Department for Culture and Social Cohesion   BERLIN   TORONTO ARTS COUNCIL   FUNDED BY THE CITY OF TORONTO

We acknowledge for their financial support of our publishing program the Canada Council for the Arts, the Ontario Arts Council, and the Government of Canada. Funded by Berlin Senate Department of Culture and Social Cohesion.

Printed and bound in Canada

MIX
Paper
FSC www.fsc.org   FSC® C100212

For Abbu

CONTENTS

AUTHOR'S NOTE

THE FIRST TIME I interviewed a memoirist in my nascent career as a reporter, I asked her how she was able to recall the many quotes used throughout the book. She laughed and told me she made them up. Young and naive, I was shaken by this.

Memoir is a form distinct from traditional reporting, and part of the territory is relying on a writer and her subjects' fallible memories to recreate personal history. And while even in reporting there isn't a single story that is the "right" one, I believe in being transparent with a reader about how a story is constructed, especially when it's presented as nonfiction.

While I'm a journalist, this book is not a work of pure journalism. It blends memoir, investigation, and creative nonfiction.

The book is set out in alternating chapters. First, you'll encounter my voice as I stumbled my way through uncovering my grandmother's story. These chapters follow journalistic rules more closely, using research, interviews, and memory to create the narrative.

These chapters alternate with a narrative from my grandmother's perspective, which hews closer to creative nonfiction than journalism. Over a period of six years, I interviewed about two dozen people to recreate my grandmother's life story. I made two trips to Pakistan, travelled to the United States and the United Kingdom to undertake these interviews, visited places she lived, and collected relevant material like letters and photos. I was also fortunate to have two detailed records of my broader family history to lean on.

If you see a quote in these chapters, it came from someone telling me what was said, either first- or second-hand. No major events in her life are simply imagined, although some scenes are inspired by partial memories and coloured in using historical context.

Historical research—archival news articles, academic papers, books, and photos—helped me fill in the kinds of details interviews weren't able to. This includes elements like what a crowded port looked like in 1950s Mumbai, what arriving in a small-town railway station would have been like in 1963, or what one might have observed riding a bus across Karachi in 1973. I have included major sources I relied on at the back of the book, including citing a few key sources that informed ideas that appear in the historical chapters in particular.

There are moments where I infer what my grandmother would have been thinking or feeling, particularly in a chapter related to abuse she endured. I hope readers understand that while these moments are my attempt to close the distance between the facts of her experience and the impact they left on her, they cannot truly be attributed to her.

While my family's names have remained the same, I used pseudonyms for three people in this book—Shakeel, Saba, and Aqsa.

Books are not always fact-checked (!), but I worked with an independent fact-checker to speak with all major interviewees to ensure their contributions were accurately reflected.

And finally, I considered many perspectives when writing, but of course the narrative doesn't include all of them in every moment. This is my attempt to honour multiple memories, and any errors are mine alone.

FAMILY TREE

Tahira's Family

Latif Ahmed Ansari ———┬——— Hajra Khatoon

Zubaida Ansari (1918–1996)

Tahira Ansari (1922–2001)

Salahuddin Yusuf Ansari (1925–1937)

Salma Ansari (died age 3)

Rashid Ahmed Ansari (1935–1994)

Saleha Ansari (d. 1991)

Tahira's Stepchildren and Children

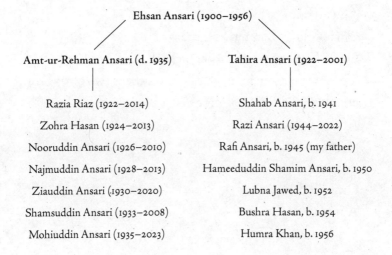

Ehsan Ansari (1900–1956)

Amt-ur-Rehman Ansari (d. 1935)   Tahira Ansari (1922–2001)

Razia Riaz (1922–2014)   Shahab Ansari, b. 1941

Zohra Hasan (1924–2013)   Razi Ansari (1944–2022)

Nooruddin Ansari (1926–2010)   Rafi Ansari, b. 1945 (my father)

Najmuddin Ansari (1928–2013)   Hameeduddin Shamim Ansari, b. 1950

Ziauddin Ansari (1930–2020)   Lubna Jawed, b. 1952

Shamsuddin Ansari (1933–2008)   Bushra Hasan, b. 1954

Mohiuddin Ansari (1935–2023)   Humra Khan, b. 1956

There are fourteen siblings in total: five sisters and nine brothers—seven are Tahira's stepchildren (and first cousins), and seven are her own children. Tahira's official documents state 1920 as her birth date, but there was no certainty about her actual date of birth. She always maintained she was fourteen when she was married, although others have said she was sixteen. In the spirit of honouring her story, I have stayed true to the age she told me she was when she was married, which makes her birth year 1922.

Names for family relations: Relatives from paternal and maternal sides of the family have distinct names.

PATERNAL
Grandmother: daadi
Grandfather: daada
Aunt: phupi
Uncle (older than father): thaaya
Uncle (younger than father): chacha*
*For some reason, in my family, my father's two older brothers, Razi and Shahab, were also called *chacha*.

MATERNAL
Grandmother: naani
Grandfather: naana
Aunt: khala
Uncle: maamoo

Introduction

A SECOND DEATH

I WAS CALLED DOWN to the principal's office exactly once in my four years at Middle Collegiate Institute. My high school was less than a decade old then. When its designers predicted the future in the early 1990s, they decided the only colours that would matter in the new millennium would be mauve, silver, and white. The stairs I came down after leaving my second-floor French class used to be mauve, but muted from years of foot traffic they approximated three-day-old puke. This unfortunate shade bled into greying rubberized edges placed to prevent slipping in the kinds of situations teenagers often found themselves in—the situation I found myself in—overcome by emotion, rushing down the stairs.

I walked down a curved hallway barely illuminated by scattered pot lights, then entered the office every student avoided if they could. A soft-spoken secretary told me that my father would pick me up shortly. His mother had been

in the hospital for the last few days, her heart disease growing stronger than her ability to fight it. It wasn't looking
good, the secretary told me gently.

My grandmother Tahira—or Daadi, as I called her—
had lived with our family since I was five years old. Daadi
was nearly seventy when she arrived at our home just
outside Toronto. I'm not sure if my father was eager to
make up for lost time with his mother, but he was bound
by a cultural code that bordered on dogma: he had a duty
to take care of his mother, whether or not his mother had
taken care of him.

Over the ten years Daadi lived with us, age deepened
the curve in her spine, but otherwise she projected ramrod
strength: hair always pulled back, fierce brown eyes, a sharp
tongue. Even her nose held a note of defiance—small and
upright, not soft and lazily settling into her face like mine
and my dad's. Blunt and demanding, she wielded the full
power her status as an elder afforded her.

We shared a room until I was ten. Her double bed sat
on the right side of our bedroom, my tiny single pushed
against the left side, with just enough room for a narrow
walkway between us. We'd both lie in bed at night reading.
My books were in English, the latest library haul or, when I
was lucky, a score from the Scholastic catalogue. She settled
into weathered books of Urdu poetry or, when she was
lucky, a weekly newspaper from back home my dad picked
up at the desi grocery store.

She wasn't the type of grandmother who would read to
me or regale me with stories of what my father was like as

a child. Nor did she ever offer to comb Amla oil through my hair and put it in braids at night, as she did with her own. With less than a metre between our beds, I created as much distance between us as possible. Even as a child I recognized she wasn't particularly interested in me.

The sole bedtime story she told me when I was very young was about a family with seven daughters. After each birth, the misfortune the family felt deepened as their hopes for a son were once again dashed, and the burden of collecting daughters became increasingly heavier. My parents had two girls, me and my older sister, and occasionally fielded questions about not having a boy, as though it was in their control to conjure the preferred gender from my mother's womb. They always responded—loud enough for us to hear—that they were thrilled to have daughters, that they never thought to keep trying.

But the truth is, my father contemplated trading me with his youngest brother's child when I was a few months old. My uncle Shamim and his wife, Saima, who lived in Karachi, hoped for a girl when she gave birth to her third son six months after I was born. My mother, like any sane person, refused. (My father swears it was all a joke—my mother's silence on the subject refutes this claim.)

My aunt and uncle had a girl eventually, two years younger than me. It was Shamim and Saima's children my grandmother raised in Karachi before our mutual accidental inheritance of each other. Photos of them being rocked on her lap or laughing while she cut their birthday cakes depicted a woman I didn't recognize. It was their daughter

Daadi slipped my prized My Little Pony to (the yellow one with the rainbow-haired tail), their boys she sewed cute little vests for (the kind worn over crisp kurtas). The only items she sewed for me, completely unprompted, were modest clothes for my Barbies, who embarrassed her with their miniskirts and short shorts.

While we were physically close enough for me to know her sleeping habits, and for her to know which of my dolls were slutty enough to need a custom shalwar, as a child I knew next to nothing about Daadi's history. About why she came to Canada. Why she lived with us. Why, it seemed, she would have preferred to live with Shamim. My understanding of brown grandmothers meant I assumed the answers to those questions were uncomplicated: she came so her sons could take care of her in her old age. Shamim was her youngest son, a natural candidate for favourite.

It wasn't until I was ten years old, when a chatty aunt blurted out that Daadi had once abandoned her seven children for a man, that I got a hint of the real story—one that radically challenged what I thought I knew about her. Left uninvestigated, this story could easily disappear from our family history. Growing up less than a metre away from her, I had no idea that she vanished from her children's lives for so long that they let people believe she was dead.

I certainly didn't have the courage to ask her or even my parents about her absence. A strict code of propriety was instilled in me early, and that same code prevented my parents from broaching the subject with Daadi even when she lived in our home. My mother didn't want to embarrass anyone by bringing it up. My father never mentioned to his children that he had been separated from his mother. And Daadi herself never offered to shed light on her exile.

As a result, Daadi's time away grew into a strange living mystery for me. Nothing had changed for her—she sat downstairs, sewing, writing in a tattered notebook, reading the Quran. But the silences I previously didn't know existed now hung heavy, carrying the weight of endless questions: *Who was the man she left her children for? Where did she go? Was it true that her new marriage lasted only a year? Why didn't she return if that was true?* I couldn't imagine asking an adult these questions. We stopped sharing a room when I was ten, and afterward, entering her quarters seemed to require an invitation—being beckoned to bring her tea, or thread a needle for her. An uninvited interview was out of the question.

But there were whispers from older cousins—that Daadi was actually my grandfather's third wife, that she might have had a secret child with her second husband, that they were never married at all—relaying what they overheard in hushed conversations between their parents. Unlike my mother, who would tell us everything, from spying on her German neighbours to recalling the harrowing night her father died, my father rarely told us stories from his childhood, let alone anything that could be considered a trail of breadcrumbs.

With such limited information, I couldn't connect the woman who only ever left our home to be shuttled to doctors' offices or her other children's homes to the woman who moved across Pakistan to begin a new life with a mysterious man. In those early stories, Daadi was cast as lead villain, an unspoken question tinting the narrative: *What kind of mother leaves her children?*

But for me, it didn't add up that the woman who chastised me so severely over my mispronunciation of Arabic during Quran lessons had coloured so wildly outside the lines of what I had been taught was acceptable behaviour for a good Muslim woman. And it revealed my own lack of imagination as a child, my limited understanding of what a brown woman could be in her era. Who was she during those years when she was no longer a wife or a mother?

BY THE TIME I walked back to class, stuffed my books in my backpack, and collected my pink shell from my locker, my father arrived in his black Nissan Maxima.

It was the middle of April. As we drove past farmland, remnants of a winter chill hung in the overcast sky, cementing the silence we drove in, my father's usual old-timey Bollywood tunes muted. I was a sensitive fifteen-year-old, but one who reserved that sensitivity for my own angst over my latest crush asking me for advice on how to date my best friend. So I had no words when regret started to pour out of my father, in what became the first adult conversation we would have.

The night before Daadi was admitted to the hospital, my father told me that when he came home from work, she called for him from her room. By that time, her arthritis made it difficult for her to climb stairs, so we had converted the family room on the main floor into her bedroom. She sat on the edge of her bed, facing the faded pink velvet loveseat that guests she courted often settled into. Daadi asked him to take a seat on that couch; she wanted to discuss something "important." He was spent after a long day and not in the mood for deep conversation. "We'll talk later," he recalled saying, then disappeared into the kitchen to make his nightly cup of tea.

"I should have sat with her then," he said to me, shaking his head. "I should have been there today."

It was the second time in my life I saw my father cry. The first time had been four years earlier after my maternal grandmother died. He cried quietly then as people filed into our home, their hands heavy with trays of pulao and daal, as if food could fill the void in my mother's heart where her mother used to live. But it was in the Maxima that I saw him sob, barely able to catch his breath as his shoulders heaved, attempting to steady himself by clutching the wheel with both hands. Vision blurred by tears behind his glasses, he looked straight ahead.

"Your mother is an angel," he told me. In another car, in another family, this might mean the obvious thing one feels when their parent is slipping from this world: he was lamenting the loss of his mother and telling me to value my own. But I knew what he meant. That my mother was an angel for not just tolerating, but accommodating, Daadi's angry fits, her casual cruelty toward her children. "She took Daadi in when no one else would," he continued. It only dawned on me then how strange it was my father always referred to his mother with the same name we did, daadi, rather than amma. I always thought it was just another expression of my dad's quirky personality rather than a recognition of a severed connection.

The ten-minute drive ended in the hospital parking lot. On entering, we were hit with the smell of illness intermingled with antiseptic that permeates every hospital. We sped down the long hallway, away from the ER and to the intensive care unit. We turned into the third room on the left, where Daadi lay still in her hospital bed, surrounded by dusty pink walls and countless grey and white machines spilling tubes on every available surface. Six more people than permitted in an ICU patient's room huddled around the bed. My mother was perched on the right side of Daadi and turned to look at us over her shoulder as we walked in. We were too late.

Daadi had been unconscious the day before but woke up mid-morning, suddenly alert. A tracheal tube blocked her speech, so she wrote a single word in Urdu on a small, crumpled piece of lined paper: *chai*. Her final request couldn't be honoured, of course. But it tipped off hospital staff that Daadi's time with us was nearing an end. Apparently, it's common for people near death to become alert, chatty even, days or hours before their time. Known as terminal lucidity, it has been observed in medical literature for 250 years, even in patients with severe dementia or other mental decline. It's a phenomenon that soap operas surprisingly get right—a squeeze of the hands, a declaration of love, and even the revelation of a long-buried secret can all actually happen.

My father got the call about her lucidity before he raced to pick me up. The speed at which he drove revealed the hope he held that maybe he could still have that conversation with her. But his tears and pre-emptive regret revealed a much deeper recognition: after fifty-five years of being his mother's son, he didn't expect now would be the moment he would get to know her.

Arriving moments after she left her body, he had run out of time for apologies to be uttered, forgiveness to be bestowed. And the black box containing the events of nearly two decades where he had no contact with his mother remained sealed.

Chapter 1

A CLUMSY INVESTIGATOR

ON A QUIET AFTERNOON, ten years after Daadi died, I sat with my parents in the room she used to live in on the ground floor of our home that we had since turned back into a family room. I was twenty-five years old, home for the holidays from journalism school, pulsing with an obnoxious desire to practise my interviewing skills.

Squished on the couch between my parents, I asked my dad what it was like to see Daadi after eighteen years while on a visit to Karachi. "Awkward," he responded. I was so used to elders being spoken about with the utmost reverence that this single word felt like a revelation to me. I asked my mother what it was like to meet her. She smiled wryly and told me the first thing my grandmother said to her was that my father was supposed to marry someone else. He looked up at her, surprised, "You never told me that."

THAT WAS THE FIRST time I asked about Daadi's time away. And the conversation that resulted stayed with me for years. It revealed how little I knew about her, let alone how her disappearance—and reappearance—impacted my family.

As a child, I believed the stories my elders told me. I had no reason not to, especially since desi culture reinforces that your elders unequivocally know best. As for plot gaps, like most children, I either ignored them or inadvertently filled in the ellipses with assumptions.

Perhaps the most vital element of growing up is becoming aware that the stories you are told and the stories you tell yourself have primarily been shaped by your parents' world view. The realization that history isn't simply recorded, but also invented. It's arriving at the understanding that your parents don't know everything, and in passing down what they do know, they can be unreliable narrators.

The latter can be motivated by many things: faulty memory, protecting the next generation from a painful past, or intentional mythmaking. But I started to realize that the gaps I was coming up against in our family history were as important as the mythology. When thinking about the impenetrable silence over Daadi leaving, I wondered about the source of this silence: Was it shame over what happened, or regret over what didn't?

All of this prompted another question: What else could I uncover if I had the courage to ask?

SIX YEARS AFTER THAT initial conversation with my parents about Daadi's absence, I was working at a women's magazine. Surrounded by editors who were interested in women's lives, motivations, and interior selves, I was able to consider telling Daadi's story. And my own interests as a journalist started to become clearer. I was attracted to digging into subjects we think we know only to discover that humans act in all sorts of ways we don't expect—like reporting on how LGBTQ+ youth find a deep sense of community at evangelical colleges. It was the opposite of what I had done in daily news, which was hitting people with the headline. I was finding joy in "complicating the narratives," as journalist Amanda Ripley has succinctly put it. This is what drew me to Daadi's story: She was a woman who defied categorization. Religious yet rebellious, fiercely intelligent yet unable to hold on to the things that mattered most to her. She was a woman who had marriage and motherhood foisted on her, before becoming a young widow. And yet, those experiences didn't always make her more empathetic. They seemed to harden her.

I wondered why her children didn't dig into her past, but it makes sense that someone in my generation would be better able to cope with what she found. Author Elif Shafak has talked about families like mine—those who have been forced to migrate, collecting and carrying various kinds of trauma with them—and who is most likely in those families to investigate their history. The first generation are those like Daadi who experience the brunt of hardship, and they often don't have the language to talk about what's happened. The second generation is trying to make a new life for themselves, or, as Shafak explained in a 2021 podcast interview on Monocle Radio's *Meet the Writers*: "You just need to find your feet and you can't look back." It's the youngest in these families who tend to ask the most difficult questions about their grandparents' stories. "I have met young people with old memories," Shafak said.

There was so much distance between my life and my grandmother's—between the choices I was able to make versus the choices made for her—I didn't feel as though her story would unravel me. For my dad, the few choices she made for herself ended up being incredibly painful—losing his mother for nearly two decades. And as my dad and his siblings aged, I realized his generation would become my ancestors one day. Honouring their memory hinged on learning about their past.

GIVEN MY DAD'S LIFELONG reluctance to discuss his mother leaving him, his willingness to participate in my investigation surprised me. One of his older brothers had crowdfunded a book about their father—by all accounts a nice, but fairly average man. I sensed that my dad wanted to pay homage to his mother: the big personality forced to shrink herself over a lifetime.

I decided to interview my dad more formally—explaining the rules, audio recorder on, intending to collect a careful chronology. It was a lazy Sunday in late February when my dad and I sat down for our first official conversation, feeling momentous even though we were just at home in our pyjamas. I was staying over for the weekend, having made my bi-monthly pilgrimage to the suburbs from Toronto, where, much to my parent's chagrin, I lived on my own. We were set up in the family room, a few kilometres from where Daadi had lived with us. My parents had moved a few years prior into a light-filled, two-storey suburban home backing onto a ravine—the home they wished they had when my sister and I were children.

It was well below zero outside, so my dad's insistence on wearing a kurta necessitated a sweater vest over the flimsy cotton. He sat on the couch armed with chai, his hair and beard completely white, heavy black frames sitting on his curiously unwrinkled face. I've inherited a lot from him— for starters, every single feature on my face. This similarity prompted gasps of delight when I was a child, each "you look just like your dad!" throwing me into fresh panic that I looked like a boy—the last thing a ten-year-old who already had a shadow of a moustache needed. But I also inherited much else from him: his terrible eyesight, impatience, and the tendency to retreat into work to detach from real life.

The room we sat in opened to the kitchen, where my mother was puttering around, interrupting once in a while to tell me to "write that down!" I assured her I was recording, to trust me—this was my job. The truth was I had no idea what I was getting into, or how to handle it. And in the beginning, I didn't handle it well.

My dad and I began by looking through old photo albums, the kind most families have shoved to the back of a closet somewhere, full of mostly five-by-seven photos, and a few four-by-six photos with rounded edges from the 1960s and 1970s. I had seen most of the images dozens of times, but always flipped past people I didn't recognize—pictures from India and Pakistan from long before I was born. This time, I asked my dad to tell me about the mysterious figures. There were so many people I had never heard of before: his aunt who left her husband after he took a second wife, his uncle who married a British woman, another aunt who never married at all.

Inside one of the albums, we found a piece of paper on which Daadi had written the birthdates of all her children. Dad's was scrawled underneath Razi's and above Shamim's—"Rafi Uddin Hamid—June 12." But his passport declared his birthday was in August. My dad suspected the year of his birth, 1945, was likely wrong. But he always thought the actual date was accurate.

"How can that be?" he asked no one in particular, brow furrowed while examining the yellowing looseleaf paper for clues.

Just as this new date of birth confused my dad, I was confused about these new characters and stories I was hearing. They didn't fit the narrative his family told about themselves. That they were a "good" family: devout, educated, traditional.

That included Daadi. She was cast as a teen bride, a young widow, and then nothing until her return to the family, when she became a religious elder. She had broken some major rules that I saw her turn around and enforce.

But behind her pious persona, I recognized a fierce independence. I wondered how she managed to maintain that part of her during a lifetime that saw the emancipation of the Indian subcontinent without the emancipation of Indian women from the heavy expectations of religion, culture, men, and well, other women.

She often employed a strategy many women before her, and unfortunately after her, have used: placating expectations outwardly, while covertly doing what she really wanted. She dressed up her demands as religious duty, softened her harsh words by offering sweets. And visually, she cultivated an image that made her almost disappear into the background: a dupatta loosely fixed to her head, donning colours a widow wears—white, ecru, slate grey. But this performance wasn't what I was interested in. It was the ellipsis in her story that was driving me: *Why did she leave? What was her exile like? Did she feel cast out? Did she feel free? Why did she return?*

I wasn't sure who had the answers to these questions, but I thought I may as well start with my dad. While almost everyone in his family is a good storyteller, that doesn't mean they have sharp memories, or care about accuracy. My dad in particular doles out well-rehearsed anecdotes at parties, knows when to pause for laughter, recites poetry as punchline. So I found it strange in those early interviews about his childhood when he mostly gave me facts, rattling off names, years, locations, and asked me to verify what he couldn't quite remember with more "senior people" (he was seventy at the time, so I'm not sure who he was referring to). I didn't expect single-sentence responses, or long pauses where he squinted, looking past me, either genuinely excavating long-buried memories or searching for some he thought were acceptable to share.

I asked him the same questions over and over. Finally, out of exasperation: *How can you just not remember?*

I REALIZED THE ANSWER to that very question a week later, when in therapy, I was asked something similar: "What was your childhood like?" I had just started working with someone new and it was our second session. Other than being surprised by such an obvious question, I drew a blank. So I gave her the basics: my parents worked a lot, I had an older sister, and my grandmother lived with us when I was young. I told her that I read a lot and found ways to entertain myself. Then she asked: "Were you lonely?"

Tears sprung to my eyes, and I wasn't sure why. I spent a lot of time alone as a kid—reading, watching television, scribbling in journals. I had some afterschool activities, like choir and drama club, and my mom took us to the library as much as she could, but there wasn't a lot of money for anything else since my parents poured their income into living in a middle-class neighbourhood. As realtors, they often worked when their clients didn't—evenings and weekends were for ferrying prospective buyers from house to house. My sister was a bit too much older than me to be a playmate, and my parents didn't like me going to friends' homes.

This day-to-day isolation was in sharp contrast to my

father's siblings and their children coming over on weekends for dinner parties and horror-movie marathons, or making organized trips to Niagara Falls or a suburban theme park literally called Wonderland. As more cousins immigrated to Canada, the reasons to get together multiplied—birthdays, weddings, celebrating a cousin finishing the Quran or keeping their first fast during Ramzan. Daadi was at the centre of these events. She was the reason we often had guests over, why our house was always full on Eid. And while it seemed like there was so much love around us, it was conditional upon feeding the "good" family narrative.

When my sister had a boyfriend at fourteen, a cousin who went to the same high school lit the spark that spread the news like wildfire. My sister was lectured by aunts, ostracized by uncles, labelled troublesome. There was so much concern about her "reputation" and how that reflected on the family. But there didn't seem to be concern about the fact that her boyfriend was nineteen, five years older than her, already out of high school as she entered it. Her actual safety wasn't at the core of the concern, nor was the boyfriend's responsibility in pursuing her questioned. It always seemed to be the woman's responsibility to protect herself, even when she was just a girl.

When my parents became increasingly concerned about her very normal teen behaviour—wanting to go to the movies, being on the phone at all hours, talking to boys— they sent us to an Islamic summer school an hour away from our house. A green-and-white striped Volkswagen bus picked us up at seven every weekday morning for two months, dropping us off at seven each evening. While that summer ended up being not as tragic as I had predicted, it wasn't lost on me that my parents wielded religion as punishment. God was a figure you feared, not loved. And to earn God's love, you had to be good.

I was ten years old when we went through that crash course in Islam. But I was still haunted by the idea I was "bad"—that I should pray more, control my urge to gossip, lie less. Daadi enforced these feelings with her watchful eye over what we wore, when we left the house, and which friends came over.

Despite vocally denouncing her own experience as a young bride, Daadi glows with pride in a photo of my cousin's engagement party, when she was engaged at seventeen to a man ten years her senior. One year later, I'll never forget how my cousin's whole body shook as she wept the night before her wedding, putting on a brave face the next day for the ceremony. I was twelve years old when I observed this strange mix of celebration and sorrow. It taught me that marriage was a duty, not a choice. I knew my parents would never want me to get married before I finished my education, but the trajectory of my life seemed at odds with the shows I watched on TGIF. The middle-school dating dilemmas of *Boy Meets World*, and Kelly and Zack's never-ending drama on *Saved by the Bell* seemed like another world to me.

Fast-forward to my thirties, when I began this investigation in earnest with my dad on that cold February day, being single became like a rash on my face I had to explain.

Marriage was half your religion according to the Prophet. I never quite understood that, and the idea made me feel like half a person. At every family wedding I attended, I fielded three to thirty queries about why I wasn't married. "You can't find anyone?" one aunt asked. (This was the same aunt who often asked me how much I weighed.)

As I looked at the marriages around me, especially in my family, I wondered why women, so often hobbled by their rings, were particularly keen to push the idea onto me. "I don't really see great examples of partnership around me," I honestly answered my weight-asking aunty at yet another wedding. She acted surprised, while her son— going through a divorce himself—snorted with laughter beside her.

The South Asian obsession with marriage is as clichéd and cringe-worthy a topic to write about as the expectation to become a doctor or engineer. But the way it can terrorize a woman in particular—no matter how feminist, educated, or aware of her worth—cannot be understated.

The unremarkable fact of being a single woman in her thirties who lived on her own made me feel like an alien in my family. I could see the looks of pity from aunts and uncles, thinking completeness had evaded me. What they couldn't, or didn't want to, understand was that perhaps I had evaded marriage. And after all, I wasn't the pioneer of living alone as an unmarried woman: part of the pull I felt toward my grandmother's story was that I had a hunch she was an alien too.

YEARS AFTER BEING ASKED about my childhood by that therapist, I still resist thinking about it. My memories of childhood seem like photographs growing sepia at the edges, darkening as I see how lonely I was, how small I felt, how small some people wanted my life to be.

For my father, revisiting his childhood meant reaching back half a century to access pain he hoped he had left behind. And it's unsurprising that, at first, he could only remember bits and pieces—it's literally how memory works. "Remembering something isn't like playing back a movie, it's more like pulling in scraps from different parts of the brain," explains the host of the podcast *Every Little Thing*, distilling the work of memory researcher Charan Ranganath.

When we access long-buried memories, it can resurface the trauma those events caused. At the same time, the emotional tone of a memory can change, become more dull, because of accessing them with a new lens. The only way out is through, but it's not exactly an appealing process. I later realized my dad may well have been doing the same thing I was: avoiding discomfort by refusing to dive in all at once.

Revisiting that first audio recording, I cringe at my impatience with him. I was frustrated when what he told me contradicted what I thought I already knew. Education was so important to my family, and yet my father told me he wasn't even enrolled in school until he was eleven. I interrupted him instead of allowing him to finish his thought when he mentioned that his eldest brother never really lived with them because I didn't think it was relevant to what I needed to know. I didn't quite know what to make of the fact that my dad's family made the trip to Pakistan from India not once but twice, so I didn't ask why. And there are moments I heard him recognize my incompetence, his voice becoming irate, sharper.

I felt like my brain was short-circuiting. Many events didn't fit within the bounds of the mythology his family had created. I was discovering that my family built their story arc on a series of omissions: anything that wasn't compatible with their idea of respectability was left out of the official record.

Only at the very end, when I stopped recording, did my dad speak about his mother. And finally, I heard a familiar story. "I think the real trouble started for Daadi when she got married at such a tender age," he told me. "That was very unjust."

Chapter 2

AN UNEXPECTED WEDDING

IN THE SOFT GLOW of an early winter morning, Tahira climbed into a horse carriage with her father, setting off from their home in Nampally to traverse Hyderabad Deccan. She covered herself in a cream-coloured wool shawl, running her fingers over the thin gold embroidery that lined it, smoothing down the tassels to pass the time on the eleven-kilometre ride to her Ehsan Phupa's estate just outside the city. Along with her shawl, the fourteen-year-old brought an overnight bag, since, like most other visits to see her favourite cousins, she would spend a few days with them to make the most of the trip. The two-hour journey first took them past her neighbourhood's streets, filled with the singsong of vendors hawking oranges and figs, then north to avoid the strangled streets of the historic centre, finally dipping south to ride alongside the Musa river, past the grounds of the royal horse-racing course while listening to intermingling calls to zuhr prayer.

The city was unlike most other places across India during the Great Depression, where wealth was hollowed out as prices for crops dropped dramatically while the British kept the value of the rupee artificially high to suit their own interests. The impact was unbearable for most Indians, prompting no-rent protests and sustained anger against the British that would eventually collide with political movements to push out their colonial overlords. But even in the 1930s there were pockets of prosperity—the last Nizam of the state of Hyderabad, Osman Ali Khan, was the richest man on the planet at the time.

The Nizam ruled over a territory the size of Italy, one with its own currency, that held on to some degree of autonomy by forming an alliance with the British. His family's extreme wealth came from a diamond mine, and he was a fan of precious stones himself, regularly pictured with a heavy gold choker clasped below a stiff sherwani collar, and multiple diamond-laden necklaces layered on top.

Hyderabad offered refuge for those whose livelihoods had dried up in the 1920s and 1930s, including Tahira's family. Her father, Latif Ahmed Ansari, had moved his family to the city of Hyderabad Deccan from Ambehta in the northern state of Uttar Pradesh. Latif set off with his wife, Hajra Khatoon, and five children from their small town outside Saharanpur southwards, a 1,700-kilometre journey taking nearly two days by train, snaking their way past New Delhi, Agra, and Nagpur. They packed up their belongings with warmer weather in mind—while winter in the north meant wool kurtas were needed to manage temperatures dipping as low as five degrees Celsius, the tropical climate farther south could reach a balmy twenty-eight degrees even in December.

Two years had passed since their move in 1934, and Tahira hoped to be making the journey north again to Uttar Pradesh, this time stopping 250 kilometres south of Ambehta in Aligarh. She had received admission to the Aligarh school for girls, a boarding school designed as a precursor for girls to enter post-secondary education. Aligarh Muslim University was the best known of the schools that were part of the network, founded under a different name in 1875, quickly becoming the centre of political and intellectual life for Indian Muslims. The All-India Muslim League was headquartered there—the political party founded in 1906 to represent the Muslim minority's interests.

That was the same year trailblazer Wahid Jahan, along with her reformist husband, Shaikh Abdullah, opened a boarding school for girls. Despite it being a time of major social upheaval, the quest for education outside the home for girls and women bumped against a traditional desire for strict purdah. Jahan and Abdullah navigated this cultural requirement by building an entirely different facility for girls, going as far as surveilling students' correspondence to ensure parents would feel comfortable leaving girls under their care. While the school opened up opportunities for girls, the curriculum initially focused on cultivating well-rounded women who would make suitable companions for future husbands rather than fulfill ambitions of their own. Regardless, it would be markedly different than being homeschooled by her father, and the thought of that kind of independence, no matter how limited, thrilled Tahira.

A red-stone masjid from the Mughal era with a lonely bus stop in front of it marked for Tahira that they were on the last kilometre of the trip. As their horses trotted closer to her uncle Ehsan's property, she spotted the stone house belonging to her phupi, Ala Bi, Latif's older sister, next to the lush grove of mango trees managed by Ehsan's neighbour. Across the road from the grove was a large lake and, tucked on the east side of it, lay the palatial home of a young nawab.

The immediate surroundings of her uncle's home were relatively desolate—a few farms and homes were visible in the distance, and the road leading to the entrance to the estate was lined with towering toddy palm trees with stout branches shooting out into fronds.

As Tahira and her father reached the house, the day's warmth was reaching its height. She folded her shawl, slipping it into her overnight bag, then hopped out of the carriage. What Tahira didn't know when she arrived at her uncle's that day was that she would spend the next twenty years there. In her mind, her life stretched before her in a predictable manner: she would get a few years of formal education, stop going to school once she got married to the partner her mother had selected for her in Ambehta, continue reading poetry late into the night, have children, and hopefully meet her grandchildren one day. But Tahira's daadi, Amt-us-Salam, had other plans for her.

TAHIRA AND LATIF WALKED through the veranda, its perimeter lined with crotons, their vibrant orange and green leaves reflecting in the brass pots that held them. They opened the double doors that revealed a large drawing room flanked by two wings with eleven bedrooms total—the eastern one for guests, the western wing for the family, where Tahira often shared a bed with Razia, her favourite cousin, who was about the same age as her.

Tahira looked up at the massive chandelier hanging from the twenty-foot ceiling, thinking of her father's sister Amt-ur-Rehman, who used to be the first to greet them in this room. A year earlier, she died while giving birth to her seventh child, Mohiuddin. While that technically left her husband, Ehsan, a widower, the matter was complicated. He had gone behind his first wife's back and married a young woman, Shurfun Nisa, who came from a poor family. He would slip away a few nights a week to stay with her, but they didn't have any children together, which made the arrangement that Amt-ur-Rehman never agreed to slightly more tolerable for her.

Despite having taken a second wife, Ehsan was grounded at home with his family. That much was evident in the ambitious project he took on in 1934: to design and build his large estate, affectionately called Ehsan Manzil, *manzil* meaning destination. He had a comfortable position translating psychology and philosophy textbooks at Osmania University, a public institution founded by the Nizam, which focused on building an Urdu curriculum to counter Britain's influence over the region and combat the notion English was the key to success.

Ehsan's intense love for languages—English, Urdu, Arabic, Farsi, and German—was unsurprising given his father was a well-respected poet. Hakim Azad Ansari often travelled to Delhi to recite his poetry at mushairay that were broadcast across the country on All India Radio. Ehsan was a mellower version of his father. Where his father stood upright and slender, always wearing the Turki topi seemingly mandatory for poets on the subcontinent, Ehsan was larger with softer features, his back slightly hunched from his hours spent poring over books. He didn't chase the whimsy of an artistic life, but he often hosted mushairay at home, and he was devoted to his father. Even as an adult, when Ehsan was paid out his salary each month, he would set the stack of bills before his father, taking a few for his own expenses with permission.

Ehsan's mother had died when he was a young boy, and when he was married at twenty, his mother-in-law stepped in as the matriarch. Amt-us-Salam held a firm grip over the affairs in both her own household and those of all her children. When her daughter Amt-ur-Rehman died, Amt-us-Salam was adamant that the family not lose Ehsan to his second wife and her family, who she felt would drain her son-in-law's resources and disadvantage her grandchildren. Her desire to keep Ehsan in her own family seemed near impossible to fulfill—all her daughters were married. The only single woman in the family she could put forward wasn't a woman yet. Amt-us-Salam told her son Latif what she had decided: Tahira would marry Ehsan to ensure her grandchildren's future. In his devotion to his mother, Latif not only agreed, but didn't tell anyone who might object to it before taking his daughter to Ehsan Manzil, including Tahira herself.

When her daadi told her to prepare herself for her nikah to Ehsan, Tahira couldn't quite untangle the emotions that formed a heavy knot in her chest—confusion, hurt, and fear of what was to come. She didn't have the courage to refuse her grandmother, or her father, who tried to explain why this was best for her. Instead, she pleaded with her phupi— as a woman, surely Ala Bi would understand she couldn't possibly marry a man twenty years her senior, one she saw as a fatherly figure. Instead, she was met with a slap and a command to fall in line. Tahira ached for her mother, who didn't have a say. Hajra Khatoon wouldn't find out about the marriage until her husband returned home without their daughter.

It was an atypical wedding. There was no large gathering, no gaggle of girls singing joyful folk songs around a dhol. Under different circumstances, her cousins might have rubbed her with the traditional ubtan, haldi-infused paste, to ensure a clear complexion ahead of her wedding day; drawn patterns with mehndi on her hands, surreptitiously embedding her future husband's name in the intricate design, or teasingly stolen his shoes on the actual day of the nikah. But now they were about to become her stepchildren, it didn't seem cause for celebration. Instead, the mood was sombre as a heavy red dupatta was placed over Tahira, covering her entire face, as she waited to hear whether Ehsan accepted the match. And in response to the imam asking her if she accepted this union, Tahira whispered, "Kabul hai," a vow that severed the possibility of a future for her at Aligarh and beyond.

Tahira was one of many girls who were expected to become women at the end of this kind of ceremony. The prevalence of this kind of arrangement had prompted the Child Marriage Restraint Act, which came into force six years before Tahira's wedding, in 1930. Known as the Sarda Act, after the politician Rai Sahib Har Bilas Sarda who championed it, the law made the legal age of marriage fourteen for girls and eighteen for boys.

But the consequences of breaking the law were minor. The state had decided to grant boys a longer childhood than girls, and for girls like Tahira, the law made no difference. In a society that insisted girls be made invisible through purdah to protect them against harm, they were rarely protected when it mattered the most.

TAHIRA'S NEW HOUSEHOLD DIDN'T welcome her overnight transformation from niece to wife, cousin to stepmother. Her seven stepchildren's discomfort was palpable, and the stress of being snubbed by those she knew so well as playmates gnawed at her. Tahira would stay up all night to sew new clothes for them, but no act of devotion was enough to make up for the perceived insult of trying to replace their mother. Her father's sister Ala Bi visited daily, carefully observing Tahira interact with her nieces and nephews, as though they needed protection from her. She eyed what the new bride bought from the sabziwallah, interrupting Tahira to bargain for the price of bhindi. And when the vendors who sold gorgeous raw silk saris and thin glass bangles came to visit, Tahira didn't have the courage to buy anything for herself. She had been put in a position she wasn't permitted to properly take up. But Tahira hoped when she had her own children, something would shift.

Five years after the wedding—and one year after Ehsan became a grandfather for the first time—Tahira gave birth to her first son, Shahab. Razi and Rafi were born soon after, in 1944 and 1945, and Ehsan's home was full of young children again. Up until Partition in 1947, these children enjoyed a semblance of the sweet childhood their older half-siblings experienced—wandering the rose garden, where Ehsan carefully cultivated dozens of subspecies, sneaking out to steal fruit from the nawab's garden, and riding horseback with their older siblings.

In addition to hosting mushairay, Ehsan often welcomed guests to come stay with them, sometimes for months at a time while they settled in Hyderabad. Tahira admired his generosity, but as his wife, it was exhausting to never know how many places to set at the dastarkhan or how many rooms needed to be made up each night, and she was wary of men in the home who weren't family.

Latif would visit often, enthralled with his three grandsons, but with each visit he saw his daughter shrink, as though the demands of an expanding household drew on her reserves alone. He pulled her aside one visit and said:

"Beta, bas tum chalo." Tahira balked at her father offering to take her home, years after she needed it. "When you give someone as a sacrifice, can you really take the sacrifice back?" she dryly responded.

When Tahira's daadi died, the matriarch who presided over Latif's whole family, some of the pressure on Tahira lifted. She felt like she could become a full partner in running the household. But the relief didn't last long. Ehsan was still very much married to his second wife, and he decided to move her into the family home. When Tahira's father realized what had happened, he asked his daughter to come home with him again. On this occasion, she accepted, refusing to return to Ehsan Manzil until Shurfun Nisa left. After a few days, Tahira took her place in Ehsan Manzil again, winning one of the many battles she had faced since her wedding day.

ALTHOUGH TAHIRA NEVER MADE it to Aligarh, the ideas conceived there made their way across the subcontinent. Muhammad Ali Jinnah, leader of the Muslim League, called Aligarh "the arsenal of Muslim India," and its students were key to gaining support for establishing a new homeland for the religious minority. Tahira's future became uncertain, like that of so many other Indian Muslims, in 1947 when the country split in two. The Nizam tried to keep Hyderabad as a separate state, but in 1948 the Indian military annexed it using brute force that sparked a wave of sectarian violence. The refuge for those who had sought stability was destroyed—and it took away Tahira's personal safety net. Her parents fled to Karachi in the newly created Pakistan. Her father was a known supporter of the resistance to Indian annexation and he wouldn't be safe remaining in Hyderabad.

While far from the new borders millions were scrambling over, Tahira felt constant yearning for those who left, awaiting letters of their arrival. The news—from those who crossed over, from the radio, from newspapers—terrified her, especially hearing about women forced to jump to their deaths into wells for fear their izzat¹ would be taken from them as so many were being raped and mutilated.

As the wave of violence crested, Ehsan also considered leaving, taking the family for an exploratory visit to Karachi in 1950. But he discovered he wouldn't be able to collect his university pension if he moved. At the age of fifty, he didn't have it in him to start over.

Ehsan had ambitious goals for his children. He would assign them occupations based on their personalities, medicine for Shahab and Rafi, marine engineering for Razi. But he no longer had the strength to homeschool his younger children. Ehsan had slowed down since returning from Pakistan. A second heart attack had left him frail, unable to sit for hours tutoring his children the way he used to. He didn't have an appetite, yet his belly had expanded. At times he was left short of breath even when lying down, his swollen ankles resting on their own pillow. While Shahab

1. Respect.

and Razi had entered high school, Rafi and his younger brother Shamim were languishing at home.

While Ehsan battled with Osmania University to receive the pension he was owed, the family moved out of Ehsan Manzil into a small flat in Gound Bowly, near the city centre, both for the rental income from the house and to avoid the exorbitant cost of upkeep the property required. The days when Ehsan could decide to buy a herd of cattle to try his hand at supplying fresh milk for the neighbourhood, or a flock of hens for fresh eggs every morning, were long over. Money was so tight that Ehsan would religiously fill out a crossword puzzle in a weekly paper that promised a cash prize to one lucky person who submitted a completed entry. He never won a single rupee of prize money.

On a late January morning twenty years after Tahira married Ehsan, he awoke feeling as though a stack of bricks was bound to his chest, his heart beating rapidly, his breath shallow. Tahira nervously observed him, her hands instinctively clutching her belly. As their unborn child gained strength, Ehsan slowly weakened. As his daughter Razia kissed Ehsan's forehead one last time, tears rolling down her face, Tahira sent Rafi to bring his older brothers home from school and tell them the news.

Chapter 3

HARDENED BORDERS

"THEY USED TO CALL him Paloo," my dad told our surly Uber driver, as the rusted white minivan rattled over a bridge on one of Karachi's ever-expanding roads. The story is a familiar one to me: my uncle allegedly played cricket with Pervez Musharraf, who later became Pakistan's president through a military coup. While the tale was well-worn, this was the first time I was in that neighbourhood to see the pitch myself. The unending construction we drove by reminded my father of Paloo—he went on to try to school our driver in his own city, who remained surly but endured this. Musharraf was one of the only federal politicians who invested in the country's largest city, my dad said, adding that before this bit of TLC, "it was an orphaned city."

After barely being able to turn into a narrow street packed with cars and lined with litter, our driver slowed to a stop in front of an uninspired low-rise apartment building: 3F-10/4 in Nazimabad 3, an address my father and his siblings referred to simply as 3F. My father and I climbed out, stepping onto the dirt road. A woman peered over her balcony, perhaps suspiciously or perhaps genuinely curious why I was trailing a seventy-two-year-old, slow-walking man like a paparazzo, camera in one hand, audio recorder in the other.

The building stood where my father's childhood home used to be. That home was one of many erected rapidly post-Partition, when Karachi's population exploded from 430,000 in 1941 to more than one million just ten years later. This wasn't the home he talked about fondly to me and my sister while we were growing up. He reserved that honour for Ehsan Manzil in Hyderabad. That was the home his father built for the family, where his siblings were homeschooled, where he chased rabbits. Not the two-room concrete structure his single mother moved them into after my grandfather's death in 1956, where they lived a cramped existence, "just scraping by," as he put it. And seven years after their father died, the seven siblings were left to take care of one another after their mother walked out of that home. That home in this orphaned city.

The sky became coated with that lovely early evening patina that makes up for the faint smell of sewage that hangs perennially in the city's air, and we returned to our Uber, winding our way through chaotic traffic to settle in for the evening. Over tea, I made another attempt to broach the subject of what it was like to move to Pakistan, what life was like in that home. But he needed a break: "I don't have too many happy memories."

THAT WAS IN 2018, my first trip back to Pakistan since I was ten years old. More than two decades had passed, and while I knew it was necessary, I was nervous about how my family would receive me as an unmarried woman who, in their eyes, was way past her prime. And, as a Pakistani Canadian, how Pakistani was I, really? I had pulled away from my culture and religion in my adulthood; neither seemed to have room for a woman like me. But upon arrival at Jinnah International Airport, I felt elated. The slight humidity of the early morning air not only felt familiar, it brought me a strange sense of comfort.

Something happens in the womb, or so a friend once told me, an attachment, an unexplainable environmental influence. Is this what led to my outsized affection for a city I was born but not raised in? The dusty roads at five in the morning were nearly empty. Streetlights were scattered and not all were lit. Dawn was still more than an hour away and the dried mud caked on the road seemed to reflect in the night sky. Dusty fragments of it whirled in the air, into the rusted white van my uncle was driving, falling in my hair, settling into my skin, and reminding me of the smell of home.

A FEW DAYS AFTER my father and I visited the site of his childhood home in Karachi, we headed to Lahore—the capital of Punjab, what people often refer to as the real seat of power in Pakistan.

The trip was meant to be part research, part sightseeing.

I wondered what I could find in provincial archives that might shed light on where Daadi lived or worked, and I also held out hope I could convince my dad to make a side trip to Haroonabad, the town my grandmother had disappeared into for fifteen years. Like Lahore, Haroonabad was in Punjab, and while it was hours away from the city, it was a lot closer than Toronto, or even Karachi for that matter. My father would get agitated every time I brought it up. He repeatedly told me there was no reason to go to Haroonabad: we didn't know anyone there, no one who knew Daadi would likely be alive still, there would be no records in such a small town—his dedication to pessimism was almost impressive. I couldn't even figure out how to prove him wrong. The logistics were a nightmare for someone unfamiliar with the terrain: no hotels, a three-hour drive from the nearest city, and nobody I knew in Pakistan had ever heard of the place. I was out of my depth.

So I gave up on the idea and settled into the role of tourist, since Lahore has a much richer history than Karachi. Pre-British monuments dazzled me, even as they crumbled. The thousands of delicate mirrors adorning every surface at the Mughal-era palace Sheesh Mahal, the majesty in the tiles and engravings covering the ceilings of the Badshahi Masjid, and the serenity at Shalimar Bagh at sunset were a kind of beauty I hadn't experienced before. I felt connected to it—it's more likely my ancestors tilled land for the Mughals than hung out with them, but I still felt my heart bloom with pride in a way I've never felt looking at colonial artifacts in Canada.

We made one stop strictly for research: the Punjab archives, housed in a gorgeous white-domed building known as the Tomb of Anarkali. Popular lore says it was built for her by Mughal Emperor Jahangir—father of Shah Jahan, who commissioned the Taj Mahal—in 1615. Legend says Anarkali was in the harem of Jahangir's father, Akbar, who caught her exchanging a smile with the prince and assumed a romance between them. Akbar had her buried alive between two walls, and later, Jahangir built the tomb to honour her. The British turned it into a church but kept her cenotaph there. Today, it houses the most complete archives in the subcontinent, dating back to the 1600s. As I went through photos, maps, arrest records of those who resisted the British, my insides wrenched realizing that these documents weren't available to Indian scholars. As someone who grew up outside the subcontinent, it was the first time I realized how hardened the borders had become. And it made the couplet engraved into Anarkali's marble resting place feel that much more apt: "Could I behold the face of my beloved once more / I would thank God until the day of resurrection."

One of the only places Indians and Pakistanis converge en masse is at a daily flag-lowering ceremony at select border crossings, one of them at Wagah, thirty kilometres from Lahore. As my dad and I neared the border, we went through eight checkpoints. Our car was checked for bombs, the interior swept for weapons, our IDs examined. Past the final checkpoint, our driver dropped us off at a parking lot a few hundred metres from an imposing structure rising from the flat, dusty landscape: A stadium stood at the end of the Pakistani side of Grand Trunk Road, which, for many years, was the only road that crossed the border.

The crowd thickened as we drew closer to the stadium. The ceremony began an hour before sunset, and while time was a loose concept across the country, military time retained its meaning. The anticipation was palpable among the thousands gathering—twenty thousand in total showed up daily on both sides. My father, who had been reluctant to make the excursion, became enthralled with the spectacle around us. As we entered the grand gate, an arch of red brick flanked by two white columns, we spotted a man in full regalia—a lush black outfit lined with gold buttons, topped with a black turban with delicate gilded thread outlining each fold. My dad excitedly asked for a photo, and surprisingly, he obliged.

There was a section for locals and a section for foreigners in the open-air stadium. We were instructed by an usher to sit in the fourth row, which, like us, wasn't quite in either category. The stands formed a semicircle around the performing space, which was cut in half by a wrought-iron gate, closed ahead of the show. On the other side of the gate was the Indian stadium. I had never been to a sports game with my dad but this pretty much felt like one, although absolute allegiance to a country rather than a team electrified the atmosphere. An aggressive hype man screamed into a microphone on a podium high above the crowd, beside a massive portrait of Pakistan's founder, Quaid-e-Azam.

"Pakistan ka matlab kya?" he screeched.

"La ilaha illallah!" the crowded shouted back.[2]

The Indian spectators had their own hype man, and I wondered how long the screeching could go on for when a trumpet silenced not only those on their mics but the entire crowd. A dhol player started up, signalling the beginning of a fascinating performance from each side. Then the gate between the two stadiums opened. Over the next thirty minutes, the dhol beat quickened while Indian soldiers and Pakistani rangers faced each other, thrusting their legs up as high as possible, landing dramatically closer to their opponent each time, and then, finally, meeting in the middle and lowering the flag for the evening.

Only a pandemic and a war have stopped this ceremony. It remains a sign of brotherly collaboration and friendly competition. But the nationalism, boosted by a healthy dose of testosterone, thrumming in the stadium terrified me. And both the earnestness and zealousness of repeating "Pakistan zindabad!"[3] confused me.

When people ask me what my "background" is, I say Pakistani, but I clarify that both my parents' families lived in India pre-Partition. My family's history is rooted in both, and it always seemed strange to pretend they were such separate places, to root for one cricket team, to pledge loyalty with the severity it seems to require. While the

2. What is the meaning of Pakistan? There is no God but God! (This exchange references the first kalima, which recognizes there is one God and Muhammad was his last Prophet.)

3. Long live Pakistan.

increasing persecution of Muslims in India is doled out as proof that the creation of Pakistan was indeed necessary, the narrow idea of what kind of Muslim has become acceptable in Pakistan doesn't support early ideas that this new country would protect religious freedom more effectively. The conflation of nationality and religious affiliation is of course intentional, but it erases the rich history that came before 1947. A history where religion wasn't always at the centre of identity, one that I increasingly longed to understand.

MY FAMILY NEVER TALKED about Partition, so I never considered it part of our story. Like most crucial, life-altering events, it simply remained an unpleasant chapter not worth discussing. As a result, I imagined Partition as I learned about it at school. I thought of it as a painful but singular event—like a blade to skin, blood rushing out, followed by healing. But the reality is much messier: an estimated one to two million dead, fifteen million displaced, entire communities destroyed, and religious divisions that have not only endured, but deepened.

My father was born just two years before the British withdrawal, but the violence was already intensifying. Witnessing one of the first major massacres in Calcutta in 1946, American photojournalist Margaret Bourke-White likened the scene to the Nazi death camp Buchenwald, which she had been at the year before. Pakistani American historian Ayesha Jalal, who has studied Partition over decades, didn't mince words in a piece co-published by *Dawn* and the *Hindustan Times*: "Partition is undoubtedly one of the most momentous events in history, not only in terms of administrative dismantling, but it also resulted in large scale displacements and the mass killings of people," she wrote. "We cannot minimize Partition's legacy."

The mass disruption, migration, and violence didn't all happen in 1947 when the British conveniently and cowardly fled. Over the four years that followed Partition, nearly fifteen million people moved, and that movement continued into the 1950s. The borders in the early days were permeable, as were people's identities. As the writer Saadat Hasan Manto put it: "Despite trying, I could not separate India from Pakistan, and Pakistan from India." He was staunchly committed to staying in India, but even he was so shaken by the violence he saw post-Independence that he ultimately left for Pakistan.

This new separation, no matter how arbitrary it felt, upended millions of lives, including members of my family. For Daadi, staying in India until the mid-1950s meant being without her parents and most of her extended family after they fled for Pakistan, leaving her without a lap to lay her head on in her loneliest hour, after her husband died. And that meant she too had to leave the only country she had ever known, the only place she thought she'd ever live.

Chapter 4

THE FIRST MIGRATION

SIX MONTHS AFTER HER husband died, Tahira found herself at Nampally train station surrounded by luggage that now represented all her possessions. The station's main building was square and stout, its entrance evoking the grandeur of the Charminar, but without the four minarets that made the sixteenth-century mosque the prominent landmark at the centre of Hyderabad Deccan. For Tahira, it was a reminder she was leaving a city steeped in history for one that was growing rapidly post-Partition thanks to waves of refugees, but still lacked an identity of its own.

The platform they waited on was wide, but she kept an eye on all six of her children—the seventh, Humra, was bound to her chest, the only place she felt her three-month-old was safe. It was early morning, but the July heat already dampened the white cotton where Humra lay. Out of the corner of her eye, she could see an argument between two of her sons, their rising testosterone levels necessitating frequent conflict resolution. She also wanted to get them *inside* the train as quickly as possible to dispel any romantic notions they no doubt had about hanging outside the train off the bars of the open-air windows.

In moments like these, bitterness rose in her like acrid bile. She wasn't supposed to be alone with them. Ehsan had been two decades ahead of Tahira, but he wasn't supposed to die at fifty-six. She wasn't supposed to be a widow at thirty-four, left to manage three daughters under five and four sons who were just old enough to crave independence and look for trouble. She thought she had at least another decade—by then Shahab and Razi would be working, able to take care of themselves. To take care of her.

Tahira hired a porter to help with the bags and he hovered behind her—she was reluctant to spend money on luxuries when there were so many days of travel ahead of them, but the children were too small to carry the heavier bags. Packing up their lives in Hyderabad had put her children's personalities in full view, a pleasure for Tahira since most days she was run too ragged doing the basics—washing, feeding, clothing them—to notice how they were blooming. Some were ecstatic about the journey itself, unable to think beyond the week of travel ahead of them. Others were already nostalgic for Hyderabad. And of course, her daughters were much too young to understand any of it. Tahira was firmly in the nostalgia camp—Hyderabad had been her home for most of her life, and she would miss the sound of Telegu, the warmth of her neighbours, and she wondered when she'd next eat bananas. Her parents had requested a few bunches of them, and she wondered why. Were they too expensive in Karachi, or would the sabziwallah not have them in his cart at all? Perhaps they simply weren't as sweet.

She would also miss holding on to the fantasy of moving back into Ehsan Manzil. The home was Tahira's only asset, one she decided to keep until selling was absolutely necessary. Perhaps she harboured hope that she could somehow find her way back to it and give her children the comfortable childhood their older half-siblings had.

Miraculously, Tahira got herself, her children and all their bags on the train without incident, and she was grateful to have a window seat—the open air was an antidote to the odour rising from the crush of bodies in the third-class car. The route to Bombay would take the better part of a day, and she looked forward to saying goodbye to India over hundreds of kilometres of track snaking northwest past rivers like the Bhima and large cities like Pune. She smiled, remembering how Ehsan refused to pay train fare when the British ran the system.

Ehsan never let the opportunity slide to point out that the extensive rail network built by the British was just one more tool in the larger British design to extract anything of value out of the country. The railway was held up by colonial apologists as a prime example of progress brought to the subcontinent, but the reality was it wasn't built to benefit colonial subjects, only those who sat atop the empire. The British insisted on bringing in their own trains (at the expense of Indian taxpayers) even when Indians themselves built cheaper ones, and then used the vast network to export cotton, coal, and tea. At first, the railway employed only Europeans, and Indian passengers were mostly crammed into third-class compartments while Brits sat comfortably in first. This "beacon of progress" quickly became the stage for atrocities when the British abruptly pulled out in 1947. Train stations near the newly drawn western border became sites for mass murder, as entire compartments of refugees who nearly made it to their new country were slaughtered while conductors were spared so they could deliver the corpses across the border.

AFTER ARRIVING IN BOMBAY, Tahira and her clan stayed in a guest house before catching the weekly passenger ship to Karachi, where her parents waited for her. Shamim was only six years old at the time, but the idea of a voyage on a ship was thrilling to him, and long after that journey he would remember the steamer's name: *Saraswati*.

They boarded the ship, which was one of three that ferried passengers on the two-day journey from Bombay to Karachi. Scindia, the company founded in 1919 that operated the route, was one of the first lines of vessels owned and operated by Indians, much to the chagrin of the British. Narottam Morarjee and Walchand Hirachand founded the company after purchasing the *Empress of India*, a ship initially brought to India in 1914. That's when a prince of the Gaekwad dynasty bought it from the Canadian

Pacific Railway Company to use as a hospital ship for
Indian soldiers. After the war, the boat went up for sale
and Scindia Steamship and Navigation Company was born
with that purchase.

Tahira rounded up her group of seven on a warm
Saturday evening on a crowded dock among families that
looked just like hers—a combination of weary and hope-
ful. The women who arrived from Karachi earlier that day
didn't look so different from Tahira: in loose-fitting kurtay,
dupattay thrown over their heads, simple sandals on their
feet. Some were making the reverse move, although most
Hindus had left by 1950—a mass exodus considering that
in 1941 Karachi was nearly 48 percent Hindu.

The steamer's three levels towered in front of Tahira as
she made her way up its ramp, clutching Humra with one
hand, steadying herself on a guardrail with the other. It
had a capacity of four hundred passengers, but most were
housed on the deck, the only seats Tahira could afford. She
watched her boys explore the ship with glee, stumbling
into the engine room, accosting the crew for stories. But
there were also terrifying parts of the journey. They were
travelling during peak monsoon season in that region of the
Arabian Sea, causing the steamer to lurch and tilt suddenly.
One particularly violent wave sent tiny Humra bouncing
out of her mother's arms, rolling to the other side of the
ship, where a barricade saved her from falling into the sea.
Once Tahira recovered from the shock of that, a close call
with a shipping barge left her rattled all over again. But
Monday morning finally arrived, and she exhaled deeply

at the sight of her father on the dock, his familiar beard a bit whiter than she remembered.

She had the relief of staying with her parents for a few days before facing her next challenge: moving into a semi-finished home. Tahira's eldest stepson, Nooruddin, was building a house in Nazimabad, a new part of the city where many muhajirs were settling. There was no electricity or sewage, but they could live there rent-free, leaving the money that Nooruddin and his two brothers sent every month for food, school fees, and the odd medical emergency bound to pop up among the eight of them.

It was a single-storey stone house with two rooms and a kitchen. "Flushing" the toilet simply pushed sewage outside, and a heavy rainfall would bring it rushing back in. In warmer weather, the boys slept on the veranda, as eight bodies choked the already thick summer air inside. Tahira could barely keep them fed—she couldn't afford milk, eggs, or fruit, so she fell into a routine of making a big pot of curry in the morning that the kids ate with roti throughout the day. Shahab eventually left to live with his grandparents, and on one hand, it was a relief to have one less charge while on the other, he was the only one old enough to help.

While her boys went to school, she still had to care for her three young girls full time. As the years passed and Lubna started school, she was able to sew to make a bit of extra money. But the additional school fees meant things were tighter than before. She thought about writing letters asking her stepchildren if they could contribute more, but she knew they had their own young families to support. It was a delicate balance, and she didn't want to jeopardize the little they were receiving.

After five years of being on the edge of exhaustion from her anxiety over money, she admitted defeat and looked to the one thing of value she could sell: Ehsan Manzil. But the property was meant to be an inheritance for all fourteen of Ehsan's children. If she sold it, she couldn't bear parting with half the income to give to adults who didn't need it as badly as her children did. And even if she did get their permission, the logistics alone of a trip to Hyderabad were daunting. The house could take months to sell, and she couldn't imagine taking all seven children on another long journey, pulling them out of school with no guarantee of stable housing. It also meant giving up her last connection to Hyderabad, admitting Pakistan was home. But her own health problems were mounting, exacerbated by the daily stress of doing as much as she could for her children and knowing it was never enough. Tahira knew then that she had to find a way to sell the house—and keep all the money.

Chapter 5

ROOTS AND TRANSPLANTS

WHAT WOULD MY OWN grandmother's home have looked
like? The first time I really thought about it, it sent a pang
of jealousy through me for things I had not inherited,
could not inherit. I was twenty-six years old, spending the
summer in New York interning for a feminist news site
(before most people understood what that was, let alone
being *Teen Vogue*–level cool). I had a wonderful editor,
Corinna, who invited me and my fellow intern to her home
in the Berkshires. I didn't understand she had asked us to
come for the weekend, not just for dinner, because I was
twenty-six years old, in New York for the summer, and not
always paying attention. Luckily, the other intern was late
to catch our train out of Grand Central Station and we had
to reschedule, which allowed me to actually pack a bag for
our weekend away.

It was the first country house I was ever invited to, and
a welcome escape from the August humidity bubbling in

New York. The Berkshires are about three hours north of the city, a region in northwest Connecticut stretching into Massachusetts that features part of the Appalachians. Tony cottage country with a vibrant arts scene, it's where writers like Herman Melville and Edith Wharton once retreated to, and where creative types still flock in search of inspiration. It reminded me of Muskoka, where Toronto's monied class (and Cindy Crawford) head when temperatures rise.

The following weekend, Corinna picked us up from the train station, and on the hour-long drive to her home she told us about the history of the property. Her grandmother bought it with her third husband, and she lived in the house in waves—eventually choosing to die in it. Once Corinna's parents inherited it, she would spend spells of time in the home until one day she decided to leave her apartment in the Bronx and move there permanently.

There was a large porch out front, with cushioned wicker chairs to sink into, perfect for languid summer evenings. Around the corner from the porch was the shower, which was open to the garden—we had to coordinate to make sure we weren't expecting company. There were haphazard additions from each generation onto the original home, gold-framed art on nearly every wall, wing-backed chairs covered in floral patterns, and old-school radiators in every room. The guest room I stayed in had the tiniest single bed I'd ever seen, made up with plump pillows piled on top of a white quilt embroidered with purple flowers with perfectly circular blooms. There was a wide-striped pastel pink rug and an antique mahogany dresser, and heavy burgundy curtains hung over the window opposite the bed. In short, nothing really matched, but every item cemented the vibe: cozy and storied.

I was in awe that my editor could set her wine glass on a coffee table her grandmother had chosen, eat off the same plates, and walk the same mismatched wood floors. In my grandmother's house, the floors would have likely been tile rather than hardwood, the mahogany furniture more formal in style, wingback chairs swapped for rattan and teak ones. It was the first time I realized I had no similar place to visit.

This desire tugging at me pulled into focus a sentiment a friend had expressed: a sense she wasn't going to inherit what she was owed. She came to Canada from Romania as a refugee when she was ten, meaning she had a much clearer idea than I did of what was left behind by her family—not just the possibilities of inheritance, but the meaning in it. The impulse to be grateful for what my family was able to build in a new country was so forcefully implanted in me, it didn't leave room for missing what we left behind.

The closest thing to Corinna's family home in my imagination was Ehsan Manzil. My father and his siblings spoke of the property with reverence, as if it was an older relative. The image of this home—a grand entrance flanked by four columns, guest rooms always full of distant relatives, a rose garden with over one thousand bushes—became a set in my origin story. It was a place that evoked rich colours like deep burgundy, burnt sienna, and yellow gold, denoting the kind of wealth other South Asian kids boasted about when they visited "back home"—ayahs, cooks, servants. It was the kind of place I wished I could boast about having some claim to. But examining my family's history of moving—cities, countries, continents—has made me realize although I have not inherited a physical plot, I've inherited dual impulses related to how I define home: a deep need to feel rooted exceeded only by a desire to leave.

My dad encouraged this elevation of Ehsan Manzil, referring to it as his ancestral home, giving the impression it was in the family for generations, when really, my grandfather had built it a mere decade before my father's birth. But I knew we weren't considered Hyderabadi—there was no sweet lilt to the Urdu my dad's family spoke, and his knowledge of Telegu didn't exceed far beyond a nursery rhyme. My daada spent his early childhood in Saharanpur in northern India, taken to Bahawalpur at seven, then returned to Uttar Pradesh to study at Aligarh before eventually making his way to Hyderabad, while Daadi grew up in Ambehta.

I was surprised to discover Ehsan Manzil was only built in 1934, two years before Daadi was forced to marry my grandfather. It was meant to be our ancestral home, a valiant attempt at legacy on his part. But he wasn't even able to live there until the end of his own life, Partition then making it impossible for his descendants to inhabit it.

Ehsan Manzil was one of the many myths that was deconstructed when I started researching Daadi's story. Sometimes a discovery like this felt like a betrayal—a tall tale told at the expense of a more complicated truth that would help me understand my family better. But in this case there was a strong cultural narrative, a Western one, that contributed to my desperation to claim the home as the place I actually belonged. As an immigrant, there's an idea I should have roots that are easy to trace, a single outfit to wear to multi-culti day at school to encapsulate my culture, a coat of arms to put on my shiny tile to be part of the Canadian mosaic.

The resulting fantasy I inadvertently created was the idea that we were from a place I could point to on a map, an address I could claim as ours—a plot of land in a specific village, a house number in a city. This fantasy melded with images from Bollywood I grew up with: an immigrant returning to vast green fields ripe for harvest, women spinning in pairs, their dupattas blowing in the wind while singing, "ghar aaja pardesi, tera des bulaae re."[4] (This also happens to be the iconic scene from 1995's *Dilwale Dulhania Le Jayenge*, and yes, I am well aware that I am not a fifty-something Punjabi man returning to the farm from London, and that my family has not farmed in memory.)

Maybe this desire came from so many others trying to pin my face to a map—colleagues, professors, cab drivers, pushing to know the origins of my brown face, ignoring the fact that anyone except for an Indigenous person on Canadian land is foreign. With fellow immigrants or recent descendants, I have the tendency to be much more open.

4. Come home, your country is calling you.

With a certain type of white person, I prefer to smile politely and say I'm from Canada, clarifying that I'm from Toronto, further naming the suburb I grew up in, as though I misunderstand what they're getting at. But people can be persistent about knowing things that are none of their business, and inevitably I am worn down to giving them what they want. Even the way *Pakistan* rolls off my tongue gives them the thrill of discovering some sort of Eastern creature hiding behind my Canadian accent.

I can see their curiosity satisfied, their tight gaze on me loosening, the skin around their eyes smoothing out as they stop squinting, as though that alone has unlocked my exotic origins. And then, an excited response about a neighbour who shares my roots, their love of curry, or the occasional comment that of course it makes sense I'm Pakistani because of a deeply incorrect notion that Pakistanis are fairer-skinned than Indians.

I used to try and add a footnote to my identity— that both sides of my family had roots in India, that the subcontinent is such a large place, that skin colour can't be determined by latitudinal and longitudinal coordinates, no neat gradation of skin colour we can overlap on a map. But that's too complicated to put on my tiny tile.

BOTH SHIT LUCK AND immense privilege can be drivers to leave a country, and in my family's case, historically, it was mostly the former and now it's increasingly the latter. As I tried to figure out how many people move countries in their lifetime, I fell into a rabbit hole that made me realize how hard it is to get a cumulative figure for migration. I knew most people are not indigenous to a place—that's what makes the 476 million Indigenous people globally so special. While many move throughout a region over generations, it's less common for people to leave their countries completely (also, the concept of countries as we think of them now is relatively new, introduced in the seventeenth century). In the 1960s, around 2.5 percent of the world's population crossed borders to make a new life, and by 2020, that figure was 4 percent.

My parents have lived in five countries. By the age of five, my sister had lived in Canada, Saudi Arabia, Pakistan, and Germany. But I never saw my parents with the glamorous aura expats get to bask in, even though there was a degree of choice in most of their moves. Instead, I was indoctrinated by the Western concept of "immigration": the linear journey people expect of brown immigrants, a straight flight path from the terror and poverty of "there" to the civilization and prosperity of "here."

Canada in particular has perfected its image as a beacon of possibilities—*the Scandinavia of North America, but more open-minded about foreigners!* It is praised for its immigration system, touted as generous, fair, and most importantly, good for Canada. A large part of this is thanks to the points system installed in 1967, which still ranks prospective Canadians by categories that predict employability and adaptability—age, education level, languages spoken, and the like. If I had the exact same profile but was educated in a different country, I'm not sure I'd make the cut. The bar being so high means people often have a pretty comfortable life at home—they truly are leaving so their children can have a different life. Canada wants to bring in doctors, engineers, and nurses, but getting accredited to actually do those jobs upon arrival has been notoriously difficult. Over the decades, that has created a large pool of cheap, skilled labour, educated newcomers working "unskilled" jobs. Although strides have been made for immigrants to practise in their fields, often where there are severe labour shortages, you still hear the stories of newcomers being told they can't be considered for a position because of their lack of "Canadian experience." It's a particularly Canadian form of discrimination: politely racist, while providing cover for plausible deniability of said racism.

When my father first arrived in the early 1970s, credentials and Canadian experience weren't the hurdles immigrants faced, partly because racism was exercised more freely. He didn't know any of this before he arrived in Toronto on a snowy Christmas Eve in 1973, reunited with his two brothers, Shahab and Razi, and his nephew Faheem. But my father wasn't warned about what winter meant in Canada: "Nobody advised me that I should not come in the wintertime—it was a shocker for me." He arrived wearing a flimsy overcoat, and the way he tells it, hasn't stopped shivering since.

My mother arrived four years after him. They were married over the telephone to expedite the immigration process and she met my father upon arrival at the airport.

My sister was born in Canada a few years later, and shortly after, my father decided to take a job in Taif. He wasn't sure how long he would be in Saudi Arabia, so my mother and sister headed to Karachi until he was able to get them a family visa to join him. After two years in Saudi Arabia, they returned to Karachi. That's when I was born, during a gap year of sorts, while my parents were figuring out their next move.

My dad then landed a job with a Pakistani textile company as the general manager for Germany and Switzerland, which led my family to Frankfurt. My father left first, in September 1986, living with a flatmate while trying to secure visas and accommodation for the rest of us. His luck at Christmas never really changed. This time he didn't even have the comfort of family—his German roommate asked him to be out of the house on December 24, when the holiday is celebrated in Germany with goose, hearty potato dumplings, and red cabbage. He wandered the streets, ending up at the notoriously sketchy central train station since nothing else was open.

Thankfully, by the following Christmas, we all had settled into a suburban apartment, where it was easy to catch the train into the city, or to the airport, where my dad would often take us to watch planes taking off. There's even photographic evidence of one such trip where we look like a PIA ad—my mother with her long, dark hair in a low bun, in a crisp white kurta with a grey embroidered stand-up collar, white peep-toe sandals to match, and the six gold bangles she never took off catching a hint of light on her delicate wrists. My pudgy two-year-old hand clutches hers, in a dress so German it's almost a mini-dirndl, white with straps of bottle green at the waist and legs, white socks stuffed into gold khusay. My sister stands in front of my mother, power posing with both hands on her waist, wearing a frilly baby pink number, white socks hiked up to her knees, and ruby slippers, looking directly at my father behind the camera.

Our time in Germany was both isolating and idyllic, as my mother tells it. It was away from the suffocating expectations of family yet lacked the familiarity of any of the places she had lived. But new things became familiar. Black Forest cake became such a favourite that it was the only cake my dad brought home on our birthdays, even when we lived in Toronto (his favourite was a lighter version from a Chinese bakery where you paid cash to avoid tax). We didn't see this preference as worldly, just weird, especially when it was unveiled at birthday parties to our peers—kids expecting a standard supermarket sheet cake.

Our time in Germany came to an end the year before the country was reunified, closing their partitioned chapter. The company called my dad back to Pakistan and there was a decision to be made: take a job in a Pakistani city three hours from Karachi, or head back to Canada. For my father, there were many advantages to staying with the company—better salary, upward career trajectory, being close to family, and hearing the language he loved the most every single day. But for my parents, in making the decision, what moving to Pakistan would mean for their children

outweighed all of this. Pakistan was an increasingly conservative society under Zia-ul-Haq at the time. The Hudood
Ordinances were enacted in 1979, "Islamicizing" Pakistan's
laws by, for instance, requiring four male eyewitnesses to
prove a rape charge. Where this threshold couldn't be met, a
woman, or even a girl, could be charged with zina—unlaw-
ful fornication outside of marriage. Adultery also became a
crime, and the punishment was stoning to death. It was the
most regressive law since the country was founded. And so
universal healthcare, political stability, and the mirage of
meritocracy won my parents over.

Effectively, Canada is where I grew up—gifting me
"unaccented" English, an innate understanding of North
American culture and a great sticker collection thanks to
the Sandy Lion Sticker Factory. All of that, combined with
this dominant, unimaginative immigrant narrative that
shaped so much of my understanding of my family, meant
my own identity was reduced to a second-gen kid whose
parents made it from "there" to "here."

NEARLY THIRTY YEARS AFTER my family's move back
to Canada, a friend texted me after reading a book review
I wrote in the *Toronto Star*. Since I was a guest writer, there
was a line tacked on to the end of the review: "Sadiya is
a Pakistani Canadian journalist based in Toronto." He
seemed furious about it, insisting, "You're not Pakistani."
I was confused by his message. What would I get out of
lying? And even if I was, why would it make him mad? I

simply responded that I was. He insisted I wasn't: "You were born in Canada."

Perhaps this man had decided my family's migration history mirrored his own, a more digestible A to B journey from India. I corrected him, then avoided him for a little while, puzzled by his strong reaction and why I was so offended by it. Part of it is that I knew I had also bought into the simple immigrant narrative—it's what made me embarrassed by my parents' accents, thinking they didn't understand the world rather than realizing how tiny my worldview was. And part of it was my own discomfort with claiming the Pakistani part of myself. I grew up in a Pakistani household, there was no doubt about that. But I didn't want to be one of those people who claimed it only when it was convenient.

The truth about identity is that you don't have to announce it if you don't feel like it or justify it to anyone if you do. The truth about my own identity is that the things that make me who I am are both my deep desire to recognize my roots *and* the deep desire to explore. Like Ehsan Manzil did for my father's generation, Karachi provides grounding for me—a reminder of the journey my family has been on and why it matters. A reminder that you can cultivate your roots and still choose to transplant.

Chapter 6

THE SALE

THREE AND A HALF years after landing in Karachi, Tahira found herself at the port again. She had far less luggage this time and didn't have her unruly boys in tow. Tahira and her father flanked her three small girls, Lubna, Bushra, and Humra, the boys staying behind with her parents, who lived just a fifteen-minute walk from their home. Latif and Hajra were active grandparents—Latif visited the children most days, assigning them reading to discuss together later, while Hajra doted over them, taking meal requests and making fresh chapatis. Tahira hoped it would be a treat for the boys to have more time with their naana and naani. But her girls, at eight, five, and three years old, were too young to be left behind. So she packed them up to take them back to a place they likely had no memories of: Hyderabad Deccan. It was time to sell Ehsan Manzil.

Hurried seamen and haggling merchants crowding the dock startled Tahira. The capital continued to grow as muhajirs built up the city, and the crowds of ships showed Karachi was becoming an increasingly important commercial port on Pakistan's one-thousand-kilometre coastline. Karachi was one of the last stops on the stretch from where the Dasht River empties into Jiwani Bay, near the border with Iran, to Keti Bunder in the southeast. The standard shipping container had been invented by an American the same year Tahira moved to Pakistan, in 1956, transforming modern shipping. But while goods were moving more freely, the situation was rapidly changing for Pakistani people. Although it was still possible to travel between India and Pakistan, the growing requirements for permits and passports indicated this might not always be the case.

After Partition, maps changed quicker than identities. The new governments of both countries created documents that defined nationality in relation to the other—but for different purposes. Pakistan was worried about the sheer number of Muslims from the region who could land at its doorstep, and documents were one way of stemming the flow. India was worried about exactly what Tahira was doing: Muslims assumed to have left for good coming back to claim their property, homes that were often given to Hindus and Sikhs who crossed over from Pakistan.

In the British-controlled era, land borders in the subcontinent weren't closely monitored, and travelling between colonies didn't require much more than the funds and ability to make the journey. The British East India Company first started issuing travel documents in the mid-nineteenth century (remarkably, with no real state authority to do so, as with many other state-like acts they took on, like collecting taxes). The British Indian passport was first issued in 1912, a document only procured if the applicant could prove they were of "certain means and respectability."

In 1948, India introduced a permit system to control traffic along its western border. Pakistan followed, introducing its own entry control for the same border. While these documents often became the first formal declaration of nationality, it wasn't clear to those acquiring them that the act itself signalled any sort of final decision on where their allegiances lay, let alone their future permanent residence. It was especially tricky for Muslim Indians—getting documents to visit Pakistan could inadvertently become a declaration of the wrong nationality. If Muslims travelling to Pakistan planned to return, they were required to apply for a permit for "permanent return" to India.

Despite the bureaucratic nightmare, it seemed entirely reasonable to those like Tahira who left India that they would be able to return to deal with property or to visit family. After all, Muhammed Ali Jinnah himself didn't sell South Court, his grand bungalow facing the sea on Malabar Hill in Bombay, instead entrusting India's first high commissioner to Pakistan, Sri Prakasa, to rent it out on his behalf.

In controlling exit and entry, permits and passports became part of the process of legitimizing the arbitrary line that British lawyer Cyril Radcliffe had drawn after spending just five weeks in the region. (He had famously never been east of Paris before being assigned this task.) A long history of free movement meant border controls were not laid out or enforced uniformly overnight—most still managed to cross without documents. But Tahira knew it was better to be prepared. Even as early as 1953, she saw how a piece of paper could threaten to destabilize an entire family's future more than the Radcliffe Line already had.

Her aunt Ala Begum, along with her four children and daughter-in-law, had attempted to cross using the Bombay route to Karachi, the same one Tahira would take three years later. Ehsan was alive then, and Tahira remembered him returning weeks after he set out with Ala Begum's family. The plan was for him to escort them as far as the ship, but upon arrival at the dock, they were turned away because they didn't have passports. Getting the right piece of paper meant making a two-day trip to Delhi, so they decided to head to Amritsar instead to try crossing the land border at Wagah.

While the right train would take three days to get to Wagah, bad luck meant it took them eight days. When they finally arrived, Ala Begum's family was looted at a checkpoint just as they were leaving the country—border guards seized all the cash and jewellery they were carrying, an unfortunate occurrence that took place on both sides of the border. Ala Begum's family had emptied their accounts to make the journey and start anew and didn't even have enough money to travel beyond Wagah. Ehsan gave them whatever cash he had, keeping just what he needed to get back to Hyderabad so the family could take the train to Karachi once they arrived on the other side.

Exhausted from their two-week journey, they used some of the little money they had to hire porters to haul their trunks across a seven-mile expanse of no man's land made famous by Saadat Hasan Manto's story "Toba Tek Singh." The narrative follows Bishen Singh, one of many patients held in asylums for years after Partition—Hindu and Sikh patients still on the Pakistani side, Muslims still on the Indian side. As they prepared to be moved to their "rightful" country, bewilderment and resistance permeated the group: "Most of the inmates appeared to be dead set against the entire operation. They simply could not understand why they were being forcibly removed, thrown into buses and driven to a strange place." Singh dies in no man's land, refusing to move toward India after being told his hometown, Toba Tek Singh, was now in Pakistan.

While Ala Begum and Tahira's cousins made it to the other side, as with every crossing, a sort of death still occurred—there was an old life they would never return to. They waited another week for the train to Karachi, one struggle behind them, another looming.

THERE WAS A CRUELTY introduced alongside the border, and it was strange to think how pronounced this was at Wagah, while at sea, Tahira wouldn't even notice when the ship passed the invisible threshold where Indian customs had official purview.

Tahira's brother-in-law met her at Nampally train station, and she felt a pang of loss as a memory resurfaced from the last time she returned from Pakistan. It was in 1951, with Ehsan by her side. They had gone to Pakistan to visit his older children and scout out what their future might look like there when Ehsan fell ill, delaying their return by months. The warmth of their family embracing them at the station then was in stark contrast to the discovery made upon their return to Ehsan Manzil. The property had been confiscated by the new Indian authorities, one of many assumed to be abandoned by evacuees. Muslims returning from Pakistan discovering their homes had been seized was a widespread problem at the time, and a major driver for the controls at the western border into India in particular.

Ehsan had joined a long line of other Muslims filing court cases to have the property reinstated in his name, while also fighting a battle to have his university pension paid out to him. Luckily, the house hadn't been taken over by another family. They managed to break into their own home, finding many of their valuables stolen. The house was in a state of disrepair, and with Ehsan's pension suspended, they sold what was left—the drawing room furniture, a crystal chandelier, an antique grandfather clock, and even their electric water-supply system. The money from those items, coupled with rupees sent back by Ehsan's older sons, helped them hang on until the court cases were settled in his favour in 1954.

Upon her latest return to Hyderabad in 1960, the city felt different to Tahira. It wasn't much busier—the population hadn't grown significantly, but Partition had changed the

makeup of the former princely state. Hyderabad had been
a cosmopolitan city, attracting Arabs, Afghans, and Indians
from the north, who often intermarried and learned Urdu.
While there were some divisions between communities, the
existing religious fault lines in Hyderabad were not as clear
cut as those seen nationally—until the Indian takeover.

Immediately after Partition, Muslims from other parts
of India flocked to the independent state, especially to the
city itself, seeking the Nizam's protection. But the so-called
police action of 1948 that saw India annex the Nizam's
territory reversed Hyderabad's reputation as a haven for
Muslims.

Indian Major-General J. N. Chaudhuri, the military
governor in charge of the state once it was taken over, was
prone to equating Muslims of all stripes as supporters of
the Razakar, a largely Muslim paramilitary force resisting integration into India. Those who were suspected of
"anti-union activities" were sent to prison, the majority of
those detained being Muslim, as admitted by Chaudhuri
himself. At least two of Tahira's family members were
among the seventeen thousand imprisoned—her sister
Zubaida's husband, Jamil, was jailed briefly, and her eldest
stepdaughter's husband was wrongfully imprisoned for four
years, until 1952.

Both were accused of being Razakar supporters,
and Chaudhuri's indiscriminate campaign revealed his
adamance that all Muslims were under suspicion, including
foreigners, stating it was "absolutely necessary to get rid of
the Pathan and Arab outsiders in Hyderabad as quickly as

possible." Twenty-one thousand Arabs and Afghans—some of whom had been living in Hyderabad for generations—were rounded up, most of them detained until they could be deported. In the end, far fewer were deported as a result of the Indian miscalculation of receiving countries' ability to retaliate.

Even those born in Hyderabad weren't protected from the threat of deportation—the newly minted federal Citizenship Act, which would have conferred the right to stay to those born in India, didn't apply to princely states until 1955. But the rules of citizenship mattered less than the growing feeling that there were some who no longer belonged in this newly created nation.

The uncertainty around who had the right to claim this new nationality also extended to rights over property—after the harsh lesson learned by Tahira and Ehsan when they were locked out of their own home, she was careful to ensure Ehsan Manzil would be left under the care of her family, not inhabited by anyone who could later claim squatter's rights, or use the power vacuum during this transitory period to their advantage. After all, just months after her departure in 1956, Hyderabad ceased to exist as a state, split along linguistic lines between Mysore, Bombay, and Andhra Pradesh, with the city of Hyderabad falling into the latter.

Tahira also didn't have a sense of how long it would take to sell the house. As the weeks stretched into months, she became worried about Lubna falling behind in school, so she enrolled her locally. Tahira's trunks were always half-packed, ready to move at a moment's notice from one relative's home to the next. They first stayed at her brother-in-law's, then moved to Ala Bi's—the same phupi who used to monitor her every move in Ehsan Manzil. Time hadn't eased the tension between them, but Tahira felt she had to pay respect to her elders. Although her husband wasn't there to speak up for her, Tahira was no longer a teen bride—she could stand up for herself. Old resentments mingled with new irritations, leading to a blowout which left Tahira looking for housing again.

Shahab still had two friends in the city, Rasheed and Bal Kishan, and when they helped Tahira rent a room, she felt relief—no longer burdening family meant she was no longer at their mercy. The pair of young men would often check in on them, and when they discovered little Bushra had been running a high fever for days, barely able to keep her doe-like eyes open as fatigue took over, Bal Kishan ferried her to and from the hospital on his bicycle so she could be treated for typhoid.

But Tahira grew tired of relying on others and having strangers in her space. She longed for the home they left behind, and decided to take her girls to Ehsan Manzil one last time. The city had not yet expanded into the village of Ramantapur, where the house stood. Once idyllic, in its shuttered state it took on a more eerie form. Tahira's brother-in-law tried to dissuade her from staying there, pointing out there was no running water, no electricity. But she was resolute.

Tahira turned the main living room at the front of the home into their living quarters, sweeping away debris and dust that had accumulated over the years, discreetly removing spiders and other insects so her little ones wouldn't panic. Her brother-in-law brought her Petromax lanterns, and the kerosene lamps stayed lit during the day since all the windows and doors stayed shuttered. The girls ran through the long dark corridors, chasing each other, making up games to distract themselves from the lonely aura of the home. After a few days, Tahira gave up. It was too difficult to confine themselves in one corner of the home, too painful a contrast to the comfort she had once felt in this place.

And soon after that, Tahira gave up on selling the property. She missed her boys, her youngest brother's wedding was happening soon in Karachi, and she couldn't justify being away much longer—nearly a year had passed since she had left Pakistan. Bal Kishan and Rasheed brought Tahira and the girls to the train station, gifting them small bags of nuts and seeds to sustain them for the long way back. On the three-day journey home, Tahira's disappointment sank in. It had been a costly trip in terms of time and money—an investment that hadn't paid off.

Seeing her father at the port in Karachi was a reminder she still had someone to rely on, and despite their cramped quarters, she was relieved to be in her own home again. The multiday celebrations for Rashid's wedding were a reprieve from the mounting stress. Tahira loved a good party, sewing matching white frocks with glittery hems for her daughters. The ribbon sparkled as Rashid's new sisters-in-law pushed them higher and higher on the swings, the girls squealing in delight.

This would be one of the last happy occasions her family was together. By the next wedding season, Tahira lost her father, who died within days of contracting a stomach virus. Her safety net was gone, and she knew she had no choice but to sell the house.

Taking Humra alone this time, she left the rest of her children with Ala Begum, her soft-hearted phupi who treated her children tenderly, the very opposite of her sister Ala Bi. Tahira was gone less than six months this time, and she came back successful. Although there was a mortgage on the home from Ehsan's eldest daughter's wedding, she was able to cash out about seventeen thousand rupees for it, which could have been enough for a down payment on a modest flat. It was a windfall compared to what they had been living off of, the two hundred rupees or so a month she was receiving from her stepchildren.

Tahira didn't tell anyone she sold the house, or how much she sold it for. And she didn't intend to split the proceeds with her stepchildren. But other than some new clothes, and a few special meals, nothing much else changed for her own children.

So where did the money go?

Chapter 7

MONEY TRAUMA

ON MY DAD'S FORTY-EIGHTH birthday, he dropped me and my sister off at Razi Chacha's house, each of us with a backpack in hand. He felt his chest tightening throughout the day, but continued working, spending the morning as an interpreter for the Immigration and Refugee Board, then stopping into the Re/Max office to finish up some paperwork for his main gig as a realtor. The pain intensified that evening, and when he started to vomit, he relented to my mother's suggestion to go to the hospital. As kids, my sister and I had no idea how severe the situation was—my parents still have a way of downplaying important things to avoid panic, while hyperbolizing little things to induce it.

After we played a bit of *Mortal Kombat* with my cousin Naved, his mother handed us each a tasbeeh. She asked us to recite "ya salaamo, ya hafeezo" for each bead, and once we made it around all one hundred, to start again. *Zikr* literally means to mention—these were two of the ninety-nine names for Allah: Salaam, meaning the provider of peace, and Hafiz, meaning the one who protects. This recitation is a show of devotion fulfilling a Quranic request: "Remember Me and I shall remember you."

Zikr wasn't new to me, but I was introduced to this particular pattern of remembrance that night in 1993. It was an incantation that called for the Creator to restore health, one that would become more familiar than I would have liked in the years to come.

My parents had me when my mom was thirty-two and my dad was forty—not old by today's standards, but ancient compared with my friends' parents. My dad started seeing white hair at twenty-eight, and by the time I came along, he was completely grey. My classmates often thought he was my grandfather. But forty-eight is still young to have a heart attack with the kind of severity my dad experienced that night. He delayed treatment partly because of his insistence on working throughout the day—the Immigration and Refugee Board gig was intermittent but well paying, and he wanted to show he was reliable.

These kinds of anxious decisions related to money made by my father plagued my childhood: putting off getting the roof fixed, ignoring a leaky tub until a crack in the ceiling below appeared, buying cases of evaporated milk on sale without realizing we wouldn't be able to consume them by their expiry date. As a teenager, I begged my dad to let a white person we found in the Yellow Pages install our air conditioner instead of the guy who struck a deal with him at the masjid. (My internalized racism aside, the deep discount he was offered did in fact come at the price of the house never quite cooling down to the degree we needed during humid summers.)

He watched gas prices with the fervour of a sports fan and had a habit of doing a tour through the house to turn off every single light he thought was unnecessarily on. We would stumble through hallways, feeling the walls for the switch, and at least once a day would have to shout out: "Dad, I'm in this room!" While his frugal nature was shared by some of his siblings, his was particularly infamous. Daadi once accused me of inheriting it, after asking me for some ketchup chips in the kitchen one day. I was ten years old or so, and believing they were bad for her heart, like they were for my dad's, I gave her fewer than a dozen. My sister's eyes met Daadi's, both of them laughing at me. (It turns out that what I actually inherited was the common desi affliction of thinking I knew what others needed better than they did.)

My parents always bought generic brands at the grocery store—the brand they most often bought was literally called "No Name." They found bootleg versions of everything. On the rare occasion we had Nutella, it was a vaguely Italian-sounding brand two dollars cheaper than the real thing, a strange mix of brown and white sugary spread. (I still can't keep a jar of Nutella at home because I will inhale it by the spoonful to make up for my historical deprivation.)

My idea of luxury as a child was being able to buy Oreos at full price. We rarely had junk food at home, prompting me and my sister to make our own—my sister would slice potatoes meant for aloo-gobi into thin pieces, fry them, and sprinkle grated cheese on top. I'd bake peanut butter cookies because even if there wasn't anything fun at home like chocolate chips, we always had the ingredients to whip up a batch. I can still remember the satisfying feeling of pressing a fork into the dough before popping the cookie sheet in the oven. Everything was homemade, a source of embarrassment for me then—it was only decades later that homemade was recast as artisanal.

Dining out was an event. Once a month, we'd go out to a new Hakka restaurant that my dad heard about—he prided himself on being a pioneer of halal dining. And every few weeks, my mom would drive us to McDonald's, my sister's high-school student card getting us a special $2.99 meal. Eating those perfectly salted fries in the back seat while knowing my Filet-O-Fish waited for me was as happy as I could get.

We never had pocket money. My parents didn't understand the concept of an allowance—what could children possibly need money for? I'd collect loose change in summers, dimes and nickels jangling in my pocket as I ran to the ice cream truck with my $1.10 for a small cone filled with chocolate soft-serve twisted into vanilla. I started working at fourteen, torturing my mother by making her drive me to my 6:00 a.m. shift at Tim Hortons. But I finally had a taste of independence, of having money to spend without surveillance.

By no means did I have a deprived childhood. But there were always questions about money hanging in the air: How much was that? Did I get the best price? Did I really need to go on that field trip? My mother tells me I felt the squeeze even as a five-year-old, not asking for new shoes for weeks after holes appeared in my sneakers, my mom only noticing as my big toe started to peep out of my left shoe.

I later came to understand our financial situation as being house poor, a condition many immigrants succumb to. Chinese British writer and filmmaker Xiaolu Guo once described the "neurotic immigrant anxiety" to buy property as a way to hold on to something to call home, knowing you can't go back to your place of origin. My parents poured their money into renting, later buying, a place in a middle-class suburb. Most years, money was tight, and in the years it wasn't, the memory of that insecurity felt fresh enough to let that fear rule our household.

It wasn't an irrational fear. In my own lifetime, I have seen first-hand why my parents felt this way. They started over when they returned to Canada in 1988, my dad studying to become a realtor, his fourth career, my mom becoming an early childhood educator. My mom's income was the reliable one in those years as my dad built his business, which went up and down with the market, the ripples from the 1989 recession felt into the early 1990s. Every few months my sister and I would overhear my dad tell my mom about a client who he drove around town for months looking for their perfect home, only for them to buy from another realtor.

My dad's heart attack happened just as he was hitting his stride in real estate. It landed him in the hospital for weeks, pausing his ability to work as he waited for his scheduled open-heart surgery the following month. There were no sick days he could take, no short-term disability he could apply for. It meant he just wasn't earning.

At first, we were told the bypass surgery was a success. Surgeons took a blood vessel from his leg and redirected the flow of blood around the artery blocked with plaque. (Plaque was always a funny way of putting it to me, as if a bit of floss could fix the problem.) What followed was eight weeks of recovery—no driving, no housework, and most troublesome, no working. But his chest pain didn't go away, landing him in the hospital again, where scans showed the newly installed artery wasn't bypassing the blocked ones to help pump blood into his heart. The surgery had failed.

Doctors took no chances with a second surgery, getting the best in the city to operate on him a full year after his first heart attack. The recovery process began anew, and after over a year of my dad not being able to work regularly, my mother was at her limit. She was the caregiver to all of us on top of the two toddlers she looked after through We Watch. Those days are what my parents refer to as the hard times.

Even having witnessed all of this, my dad's frugality during my first research trip to Pakistan, more than two decades after these hard times, struck me as bizarre. While sightseeing at high noon in Lahore, he refused to buy a pair of sunglasses outside the Badshahi Masjid, instead using his hands to create a shadow over his eyes. He had sunglasses at home, he didn't need another pair. This particular pair cost one hundred rupees, about $1.25. And he wouldn't let me buy them for him either—it wasn't about *who* spent the money, it was about the money being spent.

We mainly took car-sharing apps like Uber and Careem to get around, but we were staying at the high-security Pearl Continental, where only hired drivers were let in—a parade of luxury vehicles lined the entrance just past the bomb detectors. So we walked out of the compound to try to call an Uber. Both our phones had spotty data, but my dad refused to call a taxi, knowing it would be one or two hundred rupees more than an Uber. We ended up on a thirty-minute rickshaw ride through Lahore's old town to Shalimar Bagh, my poor dad hitting his arthritic knee on the metal encasing the tuktuk. He looked terrified, vowing to never get in a rickshaw again. When leaving Shalimar Bagh, I once again suggested we call a taxi. To save that one-hundred-rupee markup, he opted to ask teenagers hanging out at the entrance to order an Uber for us, since in Pakistan, you pay cash at the end of your ride.

When I would complain about his parsimonious ways, friends would laugh at this behaviour and, with an eye on my spending habits, encourage me to be more like him. And of course, there were lessons in how he handled money: don't waste food, buy only things you need, treat things well and they will last. But I didn't learn how to handle money from my parents, and in fact, I'm not great with it. The only lesson: don't spend money, save it. Wealth doesn't accumulate in a bank account—it accumulates from earning well, spending smartly, and investing what's left over.

My mother is a savvy investor, pushing my dad to buy a second property over the decades, but he was always too anxious about stretching their money.

In Pakistan, I realized the hypervigilance my dad has about money has roots beyond his immigrant experience. While he talked about those "hard times" within my memory, he never spoke about the most grim period. It was on that same trip to Pakistan he opened up for the first time about what his childhood was like, and my mirage of Ehsan Manzil was replaced with the reality of his family's rental flat in Hyderabad, my grandfather fighting for his pension, his sudden death plunging them into financial uncertainty, and the family starting over in Karachi in a household where milk and eggs became luxuries. It hit me: my dad grew up poor. It was in sharp contrast to the way his half-siblings grew up—they were able to enjoy the glory days of Ehsan Manzil. They had been properly homeschooled by their father, they went on to higher education, and they were able to create security for themselves. Of course, my dad has never said any of that to me. He doesn't really see poverty as part of his childhood, and never compared his childhood to that of his older siblings.

While editing a piece about financial boundaries in immigrant communities—how to create healthy ones in collective cultures—I came across the idea of financial trauma. So much of it resonated with me personally: my fear around finances, the way I avoided planning beyond the next few months, the generalized anxiety I felt around tax time. I figured I was just a typical millennial. But reading about financial trauma, I realized I grew up with this intense sense of scarcity. It wasn't just about money, it extended to opportunities—I should keep whatever job I could get, no matter how terrible it made me feel, I should be happy with what I had because wanting more wasn't just foolish, it was dangerous.

That's when things started to click for me. Financial trauma is distinct from financial stress, although it can be a product of repeated or prolonged money issues. "Stress can be used to motivate us if we have strategies for coping whereas trauma can shut down our ability to take helpful action," said Chantel Chapman, a personal finance researcher and educator, quoted in a *Refinery29* article explaining financial trauma.

The research in this area is still in its nascent stages, and most of the experts have stakes in companies that help you work through your financial trauma. But there is something there. Like other forms of trauma, it goes much deeper, unconsciously influencing our behaviours. Those behaviours can include underspending, overspending, lacking boundaries with money, and avoiding your finances altogether. "If you had a grandparent who experienced extreme financial scarcity, it is likely that your parents developed some coping mechanisms along the way that could have impacted your worldview around money," said Chapman in the piece.

Reading that, it *really* clicked: my father saw his family lose everything—over and over again. In India, in Pakistan. And he himself had to start over—over and over again.

In Saudi Arabia, in Germany, in Canada. With different careers, in different currencies. This kind of constant uncertainty can't be mitigated by a budget, or a savings account.

After my dad's second surgery, he missed a total of six months of work that year. He changed his habits: quit smoking cold turkey, leaned into religion, travelling to Mecca and Medina for umrah the winter after that surgery, returning with a beard. It was strange to see him in old photos with just a moustache, and there's a part of me that doesn't even remember my chain-smoking, red meat–eating dad. His illness propelled him into yet another phase of his life, relying on his body to build another layer of resilience.

People like my parents build these layers over their lifetime. And it turns out, once you have built resilience after experiencing trauma, you might just be more equipped to deal with it again. A 2020 study on young immigrants, for instance, showed that although they experienced more traumatic events than their peers who hadn't immigrated, they had more "resilience resources" to draw upon. And a review of academic literature on migration and resilience found personality factors like optimism and intellect, along with community support, acted as "protective factors" for immigrants in North America, Europe, and Asia who face challenges such as access to housing, employment, and education.

Often when discussing what immigrants pass down to their children, there's a tendency to characterize it in bizarrely polarizing narratives—either casting them as total victims with little agency, or valorizing their resilience, making them out to be absolute heroes who survived and thrived. While elements of both narratives might be true, immigrants experience so much more than these extremes, and pass down so much more.

As a child, I never wanted to follow my parents' footsteps into self-employment. It appeared to be living under a dual oppression: working all hours with no financial security. But the freedom of it is what made working for himself appealing to my dad—not having to deal with his racist boss when he worked at a hospital pharmacy, daily indignities compounding to make him leave Canada altogether for six years. Eventually my mom joined him in the real estate business, and in the end, my parents did well for themselves.

In a funny way, I have turned out like them in more ways than I would have ever predicted: I have found the most professional and personal satisfaction in self-employment, I have moved to a country where I don't speak the language, and I have plunged into starting over in a new city five times over the last fifteen years. I'm not as risk-averse as my teenage self might have imagined I would be. As much as my parents want me to take the straight, safe path—a government job, a pension—I've inherited the ability to start over from them, and they undoubtedly inherited it from their parents.

Chapter 8

THE BREAK

THERE WERE MANY RUMOURS about where the money from the sale of Ehsan Manzil went. Some said Tahira spent it all on zaiver for her daughters, afraid of how her limited finances might impact their prospects for marriage. This jewellery would be part of their jahaiz, a wedding trousseau mothers often start collecting a decade before the event. In this iteration of the story, Tahira bought gold sets, heavy with rubies and emeralds, before crossing back over the border. She laid the necklaces flat in the lining of her purse, stitching them in with her expert hand, while the rings and jhumke were hidden in a pouch sewn to the inside of her shalwar, attached just beneath the waistband.

There was another story told where she bundled one-hundred-rupee notes with rubber bands, wrapping them in a shawl she then buried deep in her bag, but unable to hide a glint of satisfaction on her face, her luggage was snatched, searched, and looted. Depending on the politics of the person telling the story, the source of the theft shifted. Muhajirs who felt betrayed by their former countrymen in Hyderabad were sure it was one of their old neighbours, taking advantage of a single woman on her way from one relative's home to another's. Those who had been robbed on their way out of the country blamed calculating customs officers, their eyes able to quickly scan if a valise contained treasure and spot its owner's vulnerabilities. And those who felt wary of their new neighbours in Karachi were sure the theft happened in the city, where converging groups had failed to create shared values, leading to an unfortunate interception on Tahira's way to the bank.

But there were many more whispers about a sophisticated plot to siphon money from her: a man who preyed on her loneliness.

When Tahira returned to Karachi, there was no flashy show of new-found wealth, and funds from her stepchildren were still trickling in—one hundred rupees from the eldest son, fifty from the next in line, fifty from another. And the relentless rhythm of life at 3F marched on: getting her children ready for school, laundering their uniforms every other night, cooking a pot of saalan for lunch and dinner, sewing for a bit of extra money.

The house became more crowded when Tahira's cousin Asho and her husband moved in. As inflation rose and her stepchildren's contributions remained stagnant, Tahira rented one of the two rooms to the newlyweds until they could find a place of their own. The couple became a bittersweet reminder for her of what life with a partner was like—it had been seven years since Tahira experienced the tenderness of a man's hand on her shoulder.

Her iddat[5] was long over, and there was no religious reason holding her back from getting married again as a widow. But culturally, remarriage was complicated. The infamous Hindu ceremony of sati was of course not applicable to Muslim families (and was technically banned in the early nineteenth century), but there were deeply embedded ideas about the social standing of widows across the subcontinent. For instance, high-caste Hindu women at the time often shaved their heads as a mark of their status. Outside of this tradition, even across religious lines, widows often acted as if they were preparing to join the dead: wearing white, retiring showy jewellery, hesitating to reach for kajal.

And there were financial implications. A British-era law in 1856 legalized remarriage under one condition: the widow had to give up any property inherited by her previous marriage. In India, the law was changed one hundred years later, but the laws in Pakistan at that time were based on Islamic laws of inheritance. While women had some entitlements, they were uneven—for instance, a childless widow would only receive one quarter of her late husband's estate, and in practice, if a woman remarried she could be denied any stake in the estate.

The major difference between a married woman and a widow was the protection a husband provided in a deeply

5. Islamically mandated mourning period.

patriarchal society where middle-class women like Tahira were expected to be ferried around by a mahram.[6] After her father died, Tahira felt especially exposed. Five years steeped in grief and living on the brink of poverty had a consequence: an in-patient stint in the neurology ward at Jinnah Hospital.

After Tahira's release, Rafi would often accompany his mother to hospital checkups—travelling with a "man," even if he was her teenage son, was seen as more appropriate than making the hour-long bus trip alone. Rafi was surprised at one such appointment, when a middle-aged fellow turned up to join them. The man was tall and thin, but rather than projecting poise, his body looked stretched, almost frail, like branches on a tree that had reached too far and would waver in the slightest breeze. His eyes were full of concern behind heavy black frames, but Rafi felt mistrust bubble up in his chest at the sight of this stranger. Rafi wondered why this man would be concerned about his mother.

Tahira introduced him as Shakeel, a distant relative who would be staying with them. His family was also from Ambehta, and his sister, who also lived in Karachi, had rented property from Tahira's parents. But none of her children could quite trace how they were related, nor did they understand why Shakeel came to stay with them after that hospital visit when he was apparently in Karachi to spend time with his sister.

He lived in Haroonabad, a town so small it could be

6. A man in the family.

mistaken for a village, which sat a stone's throw from the Indian border in Punjab, one thousand kilometres away from Karachi. All Tahira's children knew about Shakeel beyond their supposed familial relationship was that he was widowed and had a daughter in Quetta. They assumed he didn't have a job, since he spent his days sitting in their sole armchair, chain-drinking chai, exchanging couplets with Tahira. A lightness appeared in her that her older children hadn't seen in years, that her younger ones had never experienced. Shamim quietly observed the pair huddled together one afternoon, while Shakeel recited a few lines of romantic poetry. His mother was a rapt audience, and Shamim didn't understand why simply reciting someone else's poetry would impress her—she was a poetess herself.

Beyond that, Tahira was a voracious reader. Shamim knew she preferred both those poets who had established the forms that became so central to Urdu cultural life and also the contemporaries who were at the forefront of political thought during the tumultuous first half of the twentieth century. She often revisited the classics, including Ghalib, who made Urdu accessible with his beautiful letters and ghazals. She read Muhammad Iqbal, who was rarely referred to without the honorific Allama and was credited as the philosopher behind the idea of a separate Pakistan (although he wouldn't have recognized the country's form when it took shape nine years after his death). And of course there was Faiz Ahmed Faiz, the Marxist writer who saw the other side of Partition, and who, like so many of his contemporaries, was deeply disappointed with the resulting misunderstanding of the freedom that was longed for. These works about separation and union weren't vapid notions—Shamim had never known his mother to be moved by romantic fluff, and it troubled him that she was so swayed by Shakeel.

Shamim was too young to fully understand what was happening but moments like these unsettled his older siblings, as Shakeel made himself increasingly comfortable in their home. It was obvious to them there was more going on than Tahira was telling them: *Did they want to marry? Had they secretly already done so?* But these questions gave way to tension the longer they went unanswered, begetting new, unfriendlier ones: *What did he really want from her?* Razi, who at nineteen was the eldest sibling living in the house, became so concerned he spoke to his older brother about the situation.

Biking over to 3F from his naani's home, Shahab was overwhelmed by the financial and emotional calculus that was suddenly thrust upon him. At twenty-two, he knew they were still reliant on their older brothers' monthly contributions. If there was a new man in the picture—one who wasn't contributing financially to the household— it wasn't fair to ask them to support this man. Shakeel also wasn't making any particular effort to get to know his siblings. And most concerning was the suspicious timing of his appearance—Tahira had just returned from selling the house in Hyderabad.

Shahab asked his mother to join him on a walk, an unusual request that made Tahira's stomach turn, knowing it was time to face the consequences of one of the only choices she had quietly made for herself. Shahab led the way to a nearby park to avoid his younger siblings overhearing what might devolve into an argument. Shahab was frank, telling his mother she didn't have the right to impose a strange man on his siblings.

For Tahira, Shakeel wasn't a strange man. She had known many of those men, mostly married, who tried to spend time with her children as a way to appeal to her, men she carefully guarded herself against knowing that respectability was one of the few things she had left to hold on to, to pass on to her children. But Shakeel had not been one of those men. While he wasn't young, or particularly handsome or wealthy, he gave her the company she longed for—everything from intense conversations to silly banter. Tahira tried to explain to her son that she simply fell for Shakeel.

Shahab responded that he wasn't concerned with her choice but that he wished she had gone about this relationship properly. She should have done all the things she expected of her children: consulted her elders, respected their opinions, and only if they approved, had a nikah ceremony. And finally, he wished she had considered what this utter lack of decorum meant for him: "Do you have any regard for your own children?"

Tahira was quiet, understanding that in trying to create a tiny sphere of happiness of her own, she had only managed to create an untenable situation for herself. While she looked for a path forward, she was distracted, embarrassed, and slightly indignant at being admonished by her own son. Shahab broke the silence by presenting her with an ultimatum: Stay with your children or leave with Shakeel.

"Shakeel is my choice," she told him.

And he would never forget his own response: "Consider that your children never existed."

BUT THERE ARE OTHER memories from this single day that would alter the course of eight lives in the decades to come. Memories from 3F, where an argument ensued between Shahab and Tahira after their talk at the park. In these memories, Tahira doesn't walk out but is told to leave.

Shahab would remain adamant that there was no argument, that Tahira chose to leave. But in either version of the story, the result was the same: she left.

A taxi arrived, and her children watched the driver set a suitcase in the trunk, while Tahira helped her youngest, Humra, into the car with her, with Shakeel following.

Six siblings remained on the veranda, silently watching the tail lights dim as the taxi trundled farther down the dark road they could no longer see the end of.

THE FOLLOWING DAY, LUBNA and Bushra asked for their mother, too young to understand what the argument was about or why their mother left with luggage without them. Shahab told them in a gentle voice that Tahira was going to Punjab and that she'd be back after a few days, perhaps hoping the dramatic scene that had just unfolded could be undone.

And Tahira also hoped for reconciliation, staying in Karachi to be close to her children. She knew her eldest was hot-headed, and he had been through the most in a way—he remembered his father best, remembered the life they left behind. So when Shahab tracked down her address and turned up a few weeks later with one of his brothers from the older lot, she exhaled, thinking he had cooled down. But he wasn't there to have a conversation. He was there to take Humra back to 3F.

Shahab had already been thinking about what this remaining connection meant—he didn't want his mother to have an excuse to be in touch with them. And then he intercepted a letter Lubna wrote to her youngest sister, and he realized how much the girls missed her, and how strange it would be for Humra to grow up without her sisters.

Tahira didn't understand what was happening. How could her eldest snatch her youngest from her? What about how strange it would be for Humra to grow up without her mother?

Through sobs, she asked Shahab to bring his youngest brother, Shamim. He refused, and as one of his sisters recalls: "Cheen ke le kar agaaye."[7]

7. They snatched her and brought her back.

WHEN HUMRA RETURNED TO 3F, Razi made her a big
mug of Ovaltine milk—a special treat. At six, she was happy
to be back with her siblings, slurping her chocolatey-malty
drink, but she was confused by her mother's absence. In
the days that followed, Humra would ask Shahab and Razi
in her small voice to bring Tahira back. These requests
were often met with silence, but on some occasions Shahab
would simply cry softly in response.

Shamim started to cook along with Lubna, experiment-
ing as they went, the acrid smell of burning onions often
filling their small home. When word spread they were
alone, every day someone—a distant relative, a neighbour—would come and cook a pot of kichiri and they
would all eat the same lunch and dinner of rice cooked
with lentils every day. Humra and Bushra ate the leftovers
each afternoon while home alone, in between climbing trees
in their yard and making up games to entertain each other
since neither one was enrolled in school.

This anarchy continued for eight months. And the
adults who were available to support them sometimes made
their situation even more miserable. Ala Bi had moved to
Karachi after her husband died and brought her anger
with her. The boys had vivid memories of her husband
twisting their ears, pulling their hair, slapping their wrists,
and whacking them on the back of the head, and on one
occasion, beating a cousin black and blue.

In Karachi, Ala Bi's dour manner had intensified
into something more akin to her late husband's: Ala Bi
screaming her demands and slapping the younger children

became common. The girls were terrified of her. Ala Bi lost her purse in their home one day, and as one of the girls nervously scrambled to find it, afraid of what would happen if she didn't, she opened every cupboard in the kitchen only to have a pot lid fall out of one and shatter. Ala Bi gave her a beating she would never forget.

SHAKEEL EVENTUALLY LEFT TAHIRA in Karachi to return to Haroonabad. It turned out that he did in fact have a job and had to get back to his role as a municipal clerk. Tahira wasn't ready to leave, determined to reconnect with her children.

She stayed with her older sister Zubaida in a family-owned flat in Dastagir Colony. For money, the pair would make a big pot of cholay, get on the bus, and sell small bowls of it outside a school. She would use the money for the basics, and to send small things to her children. She wrote them letters that went unanswered, and even sent Eid clothes she made for the girls, hoping they'd wear them even if she couldn't see them fill out the patterns she so carefully cut and stitched for them.

A FEW MONTHS AFTER his mother left, Rafi was able to find the address in Dastagir Colony where Tahira was staying—just five kilometres from 3F.

But he would have to make an 1,800-kilometre round trip journey before he was able to visit her without his siblings knowing. Rafi had planned a short trip to Quetta with a friend, travelling by train to the outer reaches of the eastern part of Pakistan on the famed sea-to-mountain route that took nearly twenty-four hours to complete. On his way back through the Bolan Pass, in the inhospitable mountain range that was the gateway into South Asia, he realized he could slip back into Karachi unnoticed.

His siblings weren't expecting him back on any particular day, so he wouldn't be questioned if he delayed his return. He missed his mother deeply, but his older siblings forbade contact, hiding her letters before the others could read them. When the Eid clothes arrived, Razi threw them in a metal bin and set them on fire in the yard. There was no way his older siblings could know Rafi saw their mother without him suffering the brunt of their anger. But as his memories of his father were fading, and the loss of his grandfather weighed heavily on him, he missed his mother deeply. As the mountains shrunk behind him, and the train made its way through cities again, his resolve hardened: he would go to his mother in secret before returning to 3F.

When he arrived at Karachi City station, he took a bus to Dastagir Colony, showing up at the address he hoped to find his mother at. Bag in hand, he knocked on the door nervously, performing a silent prayer that his mother would be on the other side of the door. When he saw the look on Tahira's face when she answered the door, felt her envelop him in her familiar scent, he knew he made the right decision.

The atmosphere was relaxed in the flat since Shakeel

wasn't there. The only other person was his aunt, Khala Zubaida. Tahira was ecstatic her son came to see her, and she knew the risk he was taking—alienation from his siblings, the only family he had left. So she didn't waste the little time they had complaining about his brothers, persuading him Shakeel was a good man, or discussing the difficult position she was in. Tahira chose to be her best loving self in those hours, focusing on the joy in those rare moments of one-on-one time with her sweet son. And in return, Rafi didn't ask her what her plans were, when she was coming back, or how she managed to leave them. They slept in the same bed that night, and the next day, he went back to 3F. They didn't have a prolonged goodbye, both hoping their next meeting would be soon. Neither could have imagined they wouldn't see one another again for eighteen years.

AS THE MONTHS WENT by, Tahira tried to warm her heart with the feeling of Rafi's visit, but her hope for a reunion was dwindling. And then, she was dealt another blow.

Her mother died after slowly succumbing to throat cancer, leaving Tahira feeling more unmoored than ever. She was determined to be there for her last rites—she wouldn't be cast out of her own mother's funeral. She couldn't have imagined the pain she would feel that day in the masjid, washing her mother's body a final time, watching her being wrapped in a white shroud, wondering if her own children would ever do the same for her. Those children didn't dare look at her at the masjid, afraid of their older siblings. And Tahira was too afraid to speak to them, knowing her stepchildren would be watching her, that everyone really, was watching her. After the funeral, she made a decision. Suffocating under layers of grief of losing her last parent and her children in the span of three years, she decided to join Shakeel in Haroonabad.

Tahira with Razi in her lap, her stepdaughter Zohra, and
Ehsan's first cousin Saeeda in Hyderabad Deccan, 1944

Left to right, top: Tahira, Razi, Ehsan, Zohra;
left to right, bottom: Razi stands between his parents, below
is Rafi, to the right is Shahab with Shamim in his lap,
sitting in front of Ehsan Manzil, 1950

Tahira riding a horse in Kunri, Sindh, 1951

Lubna and Bushra in Nazimabad, Karachi, 1957

Tahira with her colleagues at MC Girls Primary School,
Muhajir Colony, Haroonabad, c. 1978

Rafi in front of Ehsan Manzil, Hyderabad Deccan, 1983

Rafi in Hasina Begum's home in
Haroonabad, March 2022

Rafi looking into the room Tahira lived in at
MC Girls Primary School, Muhajir Colony,
Haroonabad, March 2022

Chapter 9

ROAD TO HAROONABAD

IT TOOK ANOTHER FOUR years after my initial research trip to Pakistan to even contemplate trying to visit Haroonabad. And yet, once the possibility presented itself, the trip seemed to happen overnight. In January 2022, my parents decided to spend the winter in Pakistan, even after my sister and I pleaded with them to delay as yet another wave of COVID-19 engulfed the world. By then, I was living in Germany, hoping to join them as I awaited approval for my residence permit to stay on. But they set off, and as the dust settled around my immigration process, I applied for a Pakistani visa and nervously waited for approval. Two weeks before my flight out, I received my visa.

I wrestled again with the problem of getting to this remote town and fretted about the state of my Urdu—living in Berlin for a year and a half meant I seldomly spoke it, mostly at desi restaurants. What steadied me was the progress I had made since my last trip to Pakistan. Irfan,

Daadi's nephew, who lived with her in Haroonabad, turned up at an interview I scheduled with my uncle Shamim a few months earlier. He gave me the names of five men, who were sons of a woman Daadi had been good friends with in Haroonabad. I also had a photograph of Daadi surrounded by fellow schoolteachers, their names listed on the back in delicate Urdu handwriting. I hired a journalist based in Lahore to chase down those leads and told myself I had done everything I could.

I arrived in Karachi in early March, utterly exhausted. I had moved into a new place days before getting on a plane, all while rushing to put two stories to bed so I could set an out-of-office reply. I felt rushed, but I knew from experience that the only way into a story is to dive in. I skirted around this one for years, and it was time to immerse myself. When working on a feature article, I spend my days reading research, writing, interviewing, picking up fiction related to the subject, talking to friends about it, and inevitably ordering delivery as the day bleeds into night and I realize I have forgotten to plan for dinner. Usually, a bit of Netflix before bed can help reset me, but I knew I couldn't distance myself from this subject by watching an episode of *Schitt's Creek*. And knowing that had kept me from deep, sustained exploration. But after losing two years to a pandemic, I realized that if I wanted to do this trip, it would have to be now.

It also helped that since I started my investigation, my dad's siblings discussed Daadi's time away much more openly. His eldest brother, Shahab, emailed a sixteen-page

Word document labelled "Memories of Father Ehsan Ahmad Ansari," including in it the very exchange he had with Daadi before she left. And the next brother in line, Razi, self-published a six-hundred-page memoir. My father's attitude toward the trip to Haroonabad had changed drastically too. Seeing his reluctance over the years, I told him I could do it on my own, and if he ever wanted to go, we could go back together. But he seemed keen, excited even. He got in touch with someone in Bahawalpur, the closest city to Haroonabad, who grew up in the small town and could show us around. In the last four years, he'd been more determined not only to spend time in Pakistan, but also to excavate the part of his childhood he had long avoided.

This yearning to return to a country one immigrated from, even after fifty years, is typical for aging immigrants, according to Karen Kobayashi, who was a social gerontologist at the University of Victoria. "As we age, our time horizon starts to shrink and we start to think about the years that we have left," she told me when I was researching a story on immigrant seniors. "There's this longing for a reconnection to what we moved away from, what we experienced in the past, and to revisit that." It's also why older immigrants start to use their native tongue more frequently, crave foods they grew up with, and seek out games they played as children.

Part of why I rushed to make the trip myself was a realization that my dad was getting older. When I arrived in Karachi, the reality of that latent urgency I felt hit me. I hadn't seen him in six months, and I was used to my dad having a rotund belly, just like Daadi's, but it was gone. He had been losing weight rapidly over the last year, and his doctors didn't know why. And while it was something we discussed over FaceTime, it was another thing to see his belt affixed at the tightest notch, his neck like a turtle's poking out of his collar, and his white button-down shirt hanging loose even while tucked into his pants. It took the wind out of me. I felt I was watching him disappear.

Moving to another country meant I saw my parents age so much more clearly—seeing them a few times a month when I lived in Toronto meant I didn't notice their wrinkles gathering and their strength faltering. After my father's heart attack and failed surgery, the idea we were losing him loomed over me my entire childhood. It kept me strapped to Toronto for years, thinking we could lose him at any moment. My deep resentment for being made to feel he was so fragile for thirty years of my life didn't prepare me for the moment when he actually started to look fragile.

SITTING IN MY PARENT'S suburban backyard on a cloudless Sunday in July 2020, I told them I was headed to Berlin for the rest of the summer. In the best of times, this would worry my parents, despite the fact that I was a thirty-something woman. During a global pandemic? Well, you can imagine.

We had been enjoying tandoori chicken my mom had barbecued earlier, sitting in a gazebo my sister and I helped build earlier that day. Ammi looked shocked at first, and then her face sort of crumpled. My dad furrowed his brow, immediately pouncing on why it was a terrible idea to travel.

I had prepared for this, and stood firm—I told them I was going. What complicated matters at the time was that my sister had taken a job out west in Calgary. She hadn't shared her plans with our parents yet, but I knew it was coming. (It was a testament to our love for one another that neither of us ever asked the other to change our plans.)

In theory, I was only going for the summer to work on a story on labour market integration of refugees who arrived in 2015, during Germany's open border policy. It was something I had been planning to do since the summer of 2019 when I visited Berlin for the first time and reported a story about the rise of white nationalism in politics, focusing on a political murder of a pro-refugee politician. After that trip, I headed to a writing residency in Banff. The cumulative effect of the month was life changing. It was the first time I felt so much freedom. It was the first stretch of time I felt intensely like myself.

Since then, I had taken a teaching position at a college, thinking perhaps my summers could be where I explored that freedom. But throughout that year, a familiar feeling of suffocation set in. It wasn't just the job—I loved my students. But over the years, I had switched jobs, moved flats, made new friends—even got bangs—and none of that settled the restlessness I felt. In fact, it only seemed to be growing, getting more impatient with me as I ignored its call.

Berlin held a particular appeal for me: I imagined it as a third place that had no expectations of me. Toronto pats itself on the back for being progressive in a lot of ways, but there is a crushing expectation to slide into a conventional life: marriage, children, property. I used to blame the Pakistani part of me for the pressure I felt to "settle down," but North American culture is just as insistent. While my friends encouraged me to find my own way, I couldn't help but feel left behind as I saw them shack up, buy homes, exchange vows.

Berlin is a city people are pulled to in pursuit of freedom—people don't really care if you have a partner or kids, and no one bats an eye if you tell them you're in a throuple. I wanted a bit of that freedom from tradition to quiet the noise around me, to hone in on what I really wanted. And what I really wanted was to imagine different possibilities for my life.

I didn't have a warm goodbye with my parents. They visited my flat in Kensington Market in downtown Toronto on a day I was feeling particularly anxious about leaving. Instead of sharing that with them, I felt I had to stand firm in my decision, not wanting to show any cracks they could dig into, deepen. I desperately wanted to be released from the life they imagined for me. I largely had been, but I was in an irrational protective mode that hardened me against my parents instead of allowing me to see them as people who loved me deeply, even if I made choices that disappointed them.

Two days later, I arrived at the airport, with a mask, gloves and armed with two types of sanitizer. As I flew across the Atlantic, watching dawn break as I reached the continent, it felt momentous.

A YEAR AND A half after I boarded that eerily empty plane at Pearson International Airport, I started to question every bit of freedom I had taken for myself. Was I a bad daughter for refusing to pretend to be interested in religion? For rolling my eyes at every cultural norm that put women in the backseat? For moving continents during a pandemic? For insisting that I be loved as I was rather than creating a shadow life of acceptable behaviour, like so many other brown kids do to cope? Or did all those impulses lead to this moment? I had spent a lifetime cultivating skills and gathering courage to learn about a woman who also tried to carve out her own way. Could that lead to a revelation, to seeing and loving Daadi for who she really was? These questions were on my mind as my parents and I packed into a taxi in Karachi and drove toward the airport at the rare hour streets were dark and quiet to catch an early flight to Bahawalpur.

The flight was one of two weekly flights to and from Karachi—the only commercial flights out of the airport of the city of 762,000. We boarded the forty-eight-seat propeller plane for the hour-long flight, soaring past Sindhi farmland, the Cholistan desert, and then into the former territory of nawabs and nizams, who, even throughout the chokehold of British colonization, held on to their territories.

From the airport, we drove into the Pakistani army's cantonment, where we were staying in an army guest house. As a journalist, it felt uncomfortable to rely on the military for anything, but a Pakistani journalist told me the army guest house is the safest place to stay and set me up with two rooms there.

Inside, the grounds shocked me. The roads were nearly empty, and unlike the dust-covered streets we traversed from the airport, these were spotless thanks to the many sweepers at work each morning. We turned into the drive-way of a building called Pelican Hall, where tables were set up in the pristine garden for us to unwind while waiting for breakfast. The meal was served in the mess hall and would be the exact same menu for the next four days: a desi-style omelette spiced with red chili powder with a smattering of diced tomatoes and coriander, cholay in more oil than I thought was necessary before noon, fresh parathay, and chai so hot you could finish your meal before touching it and still be blowing on it before taking your first sip.

Given the unstable childhood my dad and his siblings had, it surprised me that none of them ended up in the military— seemingly the only Pakistani institution with job stability. But even the tiny slice of exposure over a few days revealed that the army was yet another expression of the extreme ineq-uity present throughout the country. For those with power, it opens up new outlets for comfort and influence. The army owned royal palaces in Bahawalpur, and only one was open to the public. A military-escorted tour we somehow found ourselves on revealed that at least one of these palaces was also a guest house for high-ranking personnel, dripping with opulent crystal chandeliers, gilded picture frames, and finely woven rugs. For poor kids from remote areas, the army is one way out of poverty—but it doesn't always get them very far. The chowkidar in charge of our guest house was on call twenty-four hours a day, every single day.

My parents were shattered from the early flight, so I set off without them with the journalist who helped set up the interviews for our first talk with Rao Shujaat Ali Khan, the son of Daadi's friend Hasina Begum. He waited outside his home so I'd spot him: tall and lean in a beige kurta, nearly bald with a black moustache and kind brown eyes. He was immediately welcoming, and his bubbly wife started talking about "Khala Tahira."

"My mother made your grandmother her sister," he told me, which is why they called her khala.

His house help filled the glass-topped coffee table with mini samosas, spring rolls, chicken nuggets, and dumplings in yogourt, served with juice and chai, and over an hour and a half, a stranger filled me in on the dark stretch of time Daadi's own children knew nothing about. From him I learned that Daadi was not only a close family friend, but helped raise him and his brothers. He spoke with emotion about her, about the troubles she had with Shakeel, and how Hasina Begum was one of the few people Daadi spoke with about her own children. When we left, Shujaat's wife pressed a five-hundred-rupee note into my hand, as if I were close family visiting.

When heading back to the army compound, I wrestled with how much to tell my dad, whether it would help him to know some details ahead of our trip or if it would already be too overwhelming. We would be spending most of the following day with Shujaat's brother in Haroonabad. How would my father react to learning that instead of raising him, Daadi had raised another set of siblings?

I was reminded of a tape he used to play in the car growing up—a recorded sermon from Friday prayer by a Guyanese imam. Every time my father pushed the cassette into the dashboard's audio system, my sister and I would exchange a glance, and then the imam's melodic English would admonish his listeners for not treating their parents with the respect they deserved. In the backseat of our champagne-beige Oldsmobile 88, it felt like a typically desi—but this time outsourced—parental guilt trip. But I started to see it differently as I was confronted with the details of my father losing his parents. Unlike some of his siblings, he never spoke bitterly about either of them. And while digging into this research, sometimes I could see the little boy in him, hoping his mother had been kept away rather than had stayed away by choice. I didn't know if getting deeper into her time away would affect his ability to tell that story to himself.

That night, a mixture of uncertainty, grief, and exhaustion led to an emotional collapse of sorts. I sobbed uncontrollably as I tiptoed into my parents' room, and for the first time since I was a child, I asked my mother to hold me until I fell asleep.

WE WERE UP BEFORE dawn the next morning, and while that day started and ended in the dark as every single day does, it changed something in me.

It was a cool morning as we waited for our ride to the mess hall for our standard military breakfast. We set out for Haroonabad from Bahawalpur shortly after seven, and left the city limits within minutes, enveloped by Punjab's rural landscape, often called the breadbasket of the country. Parts of the journey were idyllic: passing endless fields of wheat and cotton, getting held up by a herd of sheep, watching cows find their spot in the sun to lie in. But there was a nervous energy we carried that didn't allow me to admire it all.

We arrived as the day was finding its strength at ten o'clock, passing beneath a large green banner declaring "Welcome Haroonabad." Our only instructions were to turn into the first gas station on the right after driving past that sign, and to tell someone there to take us to Rao Wajahat Ali Khan's home. We saw a green and white Byco sign and turned in, and when we asked for Wajahat, a teenage boy got on a red motorbike and told us to follow him.

We continued on Haroonabad's arterial road, turning into a web of smaller streets until we arrived at Wajahat's home at the end of an alley with a grand teak gate. He was waiting for us outside the gate. Like his brother, he was a tall, bald man, and he extended the same hospitality to us immediately. He had a strong moustache much like the one my dad used to sport and was in an immaculate dark grey kurta pyjama. We greeted his wife and settled in their living room—a large rectangular room with white tile and sofas lining every single wall. Cross-legged, one foot out of his black chappal, Wajahat took a seat and invited my father to sit on the large sofa next to him. He had taken the day off work to support us with our project, treating us like family, sight unseen.

Wajahat looked at me and my father and said he could see Khala Tahira in us. His eyes became glassy when mentioning her name, and after waiting so many decades for someone to arrive and ask about her, he didn't waste any more time—he dove into everything he knew about Daadi, starting with her arrival in Haroonabad.

Chapter 10

THE SECOND MIGRATION

TAHIRA HAD BEEN NERVOUS about travelling to the Haroonabad railway station on her own, but upon arrival, she realized that it was one of the last stops on the sole line that ran through the town—there were no crowds, no other platforms to criss-cross, no real way to get lost. She spotted Shakeel, waving at her just beyond the entrance, as a porter carried her trunk behind her. She glanced at the welcome sign: Population 22,000. The whole town was likely smaller than her Karachi neighbourhood, despite Nazimabad being developed only a decade earlier.

She was grateful to be off the train itself—as it carried her farther from her children, the gravity of her situation started to set in. At first, Tahira thought of her disagreement with Shahab as a fissure. But over the months Tahira sat waiting in the rented flat in Karachi, she came to realize the disagreement was actually a crack: a rock that has been split in two.

Tahira peered outside the station at the town, which lay somewhere between desert and rich agricultural land. There were no rocks in sight here, and she smiled wryly thinking of Hyderabad's famous pathar dil, a formation of boulders named heart of stone, wondering if anyone's heart could really be that impenetrable.

Tahira didn't know if leaving Karachi had been the right decision, but Islam said marriage was half her religion, so she was there to fulfill that half. It was a way to start over without feeling constant burning shame as neighbours glanced at her without saying hello, assuming only a woman with a pathar dil could leave her family.

The occasional open field with grazing cows gave her another flashback to Hyderabad, to Ehsan Manzil, but Tahira knew this was new territory. The main road was covered in dust, quiet save for a few bicycles and chai stands postered with Tapal tea advertisements. There was no nearby metropolis to disappear into.

They got out of their taxi outside a home with an imposing entrance: double wooden doors, each etched with an intricate star-like pattern. The doors were set in a slim brick facade nestled between two other homes, each built in a different style. Setting her trunk down behind him, Shakeel jiggled a skeleton key into the lock. Tahira tried to ignore the chickens clucking at the entrance, making her way around them and inside her new home.

Like 3F in Nazimabad, it was modest, with just two rooms and a large veranda. Even so, it felt empty enough to hear echoes in those early days, so Tahira threw herself

into a new routine to make it feel like home—scrubbing
the kitchen after breakfast, sweeping both rooms, wringing
out laundry, then watching the clock until it was time to
prepare dinner. She decided to take this new-found time to
devote herself to being a wife—mending Shakeel's clothes,
keeping herself attractive as a new bride by sewing smart
designs for herself, making special meals like filling keralay
with qeema, and on special occasions frying day-old bread,
then coating it with saffron syrup to make shahi tukray.

Despite her efforts to create busywork, there was an
uncomfortable stillness in the home. Tahira had never experienced this kind of silence—the lone sabziwallah selling
his wares along her street around ten o'clock in the morning
was quaint compared with the competing calls she'd hear
in 3F. And Tahira had always lived among the clutter and
chatter of a large family, not to mention the laughter, tears,
and demands of children omnipresent in every stage of her
life. Her new marriage came with a new kind of loneliness.

The moment Tahira looked forward to most came after
her daily chores in the late afternoon, when she would sit
with chai to reread volumes of poetry Shakeel had on his
shelves. As she revisited Faiz Ahmed Faiz's famous poem
"Subh-e-Azaadi," about his disenchantments with the type
of freedom Partition resulted in, she was alarmed to find it
resonated with her more deeply with each reading.

Yeh daagh daagh ujaalaa, yeh shab gazidaa seher
Woh intezaar tha jiska, yeh woh seher to nahin
Yeh woh seher to nahin, jis ki aarzoo lekar

The light, smeared and spotted, this night-bitten dawn
This isn't surely the dawn we waited for so eagerly
This isn't surely the dawn with whose desire cradled in
our hearts

HAROONABAD GAVE TAHIRA THE blank slate she needed,
but she felt empty instead of free. With her parents gone
and her remaining family keeping their distance, she was
unmoored without the relations that defined her. What
should she say in those inevitable introductory conversations that evolved into prodding into who her father was,
what town they were from in Uttar Pradesh, and all the
other details that proved she was from good stock? Was
she still allowed to claim it?

Tahira decided her lineage was still hers, getting in
touch with a distant relative who then helped fill out her
social life, introducing her to fellow Urdu-speaking families in town who had come over after Partition. There was
another woman who was also from Saharanpur, Hasina
Begum, who like Tahira, was widowed at a young age and
had been taking care of her five boys on her own ever since.
She practised strict purdah, never leaving her home, so to
meet her Tahira would have to make the pilgrimage to her
haveli. She walked over one evening, invited along with her
relatives, curious about what life in total purdah in such a
small town would be like—there didn't appear to be much
to be protected from.

Shaukat Manzil was just a few minutes' walk from Tahira's own home, but entering through the tall doors opened up another world: a large courtyard revealing three stories, the smell of almonds toasting travelling from the kitchen, and the sound of a young boy laughing while another chased him down the stairs meeting her at the entrance. The young boy stopped abruptly when he saw her, instinctively straightening the hem of his kurta, looking at her shyly. He was a few years younger than her youngest and, like Humra, born the same year his father died. Tahira crouched down to tell him her name, and just as she was about to ask his, Hasina Begum appeared.

She ushered Tahira into a room off the courtyard, and as her maid filled a table with tea and three different kinds of biscuits, Tahira learned the names of her host's five sons: Farhat Ali Khan, Shujaat, Shafaat, Shafqat, and the youngest, whom she already met, Wajahat. Hasina Begum was at least a decade younger than Tahira, but she carried herself with the weight of an elder, an unfortunate side effect of being married at fifteen and widowed before she even turned twenty-five. While Hasina Begum had arrived in Haroonabad after Partition, her husband had family connections during the nawab's heyday, securing land after being tipped off about an auction years before the split. They had done well as zamindaars, taking the profits to start another business that her boys would run in parallel. Hasina Begum's husband left behind a comfortable life for his family, an entirely alien concept to Tahira. But what her family had lacked in financial legacy they made up for in another way: education. Tahira discovered that in this small town she held a rare and powerful position as a woman who was not only literate, but spoke multiple languages and held strong opinions on everything from politics to cooking methods.

While Tahira was known as a poetess, Hasina Begum couldn't read or write. But Hasina Begum also wielded a quiet power: behind the woman in the plain white kurta pyjama, always with a dupatta over her head, often with a tasbeeh between her fingers, was someone who made connections by whispering her late husband's name. She had the kind of wealth and standing that meant she could make things happen—jobs, marriages, divorces—all from inside her compound. And she had other ethereal qualities Tahira would learn about: her dreams were sometimes premonitions, she often knew the feeling that lay in Tahira's heart, speaking to her troubles before Tahira had a chance to express them.

Despite her gifts, losing her husband in 1960 was a setback Hasina Begum never quite recovered from. She had disconnected from earthly matters like household affairs, and could only devote herself to God. There were servants to help with the housework, but Hasina Begum relied on the help of other women in the community to do things like grocery shopping. This is how Tahira came to meet many other women in the town, some of whom took turns staying with Hasina Begum, since she disliked sleeping alone.

As their friendship deepened, Tahira established a new

daily routine: she would prepare dinner for the evening, clean up after herself, then head to Hasina Begum's haveli. They would recite naatain, consider lessons from Hadith, and then Tahira would read to Hasina Begum and the children from a serial she brought. For Tahira, it was simultaneously joyful and heart-wrenching to be in the presence of children again, especially Hasina Begum's youngest, Wajahat, who grew more and more attached her. As the months went on, Tahira started to stretch her time at Hasina Begum's, leaving it until the last possible moment to return to her empty home to wait for Shakeel.

But soon, her husband began arriving home before her, and soon after that, Shakeel lacked the patience to wait for Tahira, rapping his knuckles on Hasina Begum's door to summon his wife. Hasina Begum noticed how her companion changed throughout the day, blooming when she entered the haveli, energized by the yellow, pink, and green walls of the courtyard, bursting with ideas for sewing projects and new recipes she wanted the boys to try. As time crept closer to returning home, Tahira seemed to wither, anxious about her dual desire to be home to avoid a row and to stay for herself. She didn't have to tell Hasina Begum she was having difficulties in her new marriage for her friend to realize Tahira was a woman on edge.

It was difficult to pinpoint the moment when Tahira's husband morphed from someone whose strength she leaned on into someone whose heft might suffocate her. She barely remembered the version of herself from the early days of her marriage, when she vibrated with longing for the moment she heard Shakeel's heavy steps at the door, his key turning in the lock. Over the years, that anticipation had turned into dread. She wasn't sure exactly when Shakeel stopped being a balm for the aching loneliness of not knowing how her children were, or if she'd see them again. At first, it seemed they had this in common—Shakeel also had a daughter, raised by her mother's family in Quetta. But she observed he rarely made the nine-hundred-kilometre journey to visit her in the years they had been married. And she learned Shakeel had chosen for his daughter to be raised away from him. He had never been a father in the way she had been a mother.

Their nights of sharing poetry were replaced by her becoming an audience to his recitations. One-way transmissions were preferable to conversations that held the threat of turning his mood—mentioning Hasina Begum or asking for a bit of extra money for a special meal could ruin an evening. Small digs became open hostility without warning, and along with piling on complaints, he seemed to come up with new demands each day. One in particular made Tahira balk—that she should be devoted to him alone.

As Shakeel repeatedly asked her to stop seeing Haseena, Tahira could feel rage gathering in her. She had already ripped herself from her children for this man, proving her devotion. She hadn't imagined it was possible to ask for more. So Tahira started to defy him in small ways—preparing elaborate dishes that she enjoyed more than he did, folding his clothes when they were slightly damp so they would take on a mouldy stench, misplacing his favourite poetry volumes. It didn't go unnoticed. The more Shakeel felt her resistance, the less he cared about keeping up appearances of a functional let alone happy marriage with his neighbours. His booming voice was heard nightly through the walls, residents on both sides concerned but not wanting to meddle, thinking the kindest thing they could do was pretend they were hard of hearing.

Tahira wasn't someone who could be controlled. In her first marriage, despite Ehsan being so much older than her, she argued as his equal, unafraid to push back. But Ehsan was a different type of man. She hadn't feared him.

With Shakeel, she mostly resisted by continuing to cultivate her relationship with Hasina Begum, having the prescient wisdom to ensure she had someone else to rely on. One evening when Shakeel came to collect her from Hasina Begum's, Tahira could see a pulsing anger behind his strained smile. She tried to calm him down on their walk home, telling him how she spent hours that afternoon making koftay for him: grinding meat, adding a delicate mix of spices, shaping the meatballs, and then simmering them until fully cooked to keep the beef soft. He was quiet while she gave her nervous speech, but when they arrived home, he went straight to the kitchen, took the whole pot and threw it across their front yard. The neighbour's children, who were outside playing, froze, the two little girls standing aghast. They were used to hearing Shakeel's incessant yelling through their thin walls, but the waste of beef and the rich saalan seemed criminal.

Tahira finally confessed to Hasina Begum—all her other neighbours knew what was happening anyway, she had nothing left to lose. Hasina Begum then started calling on Tahira to stay overnight, under the auspices of needing help with her children. And then Tahira started to spend nights there when the fights with Shakeel escalated into screaming matches. And when Shakeel's abuse became unbearable, Hasina Begum sent a paigham[8] out to her cousins: *He's creating trouble for Tahira. Do something about him.*

Tahira didn't know what the message meant exactly. While she didn't want Shakeel to be physically harmed, she wanted him to feel the terror he filled her with, even if she couldn't punish him the way he had punished her—hollowing out her life to make sure she would be left with nothing but this fear. After a few of these messages were sent, even Tahira could see the pattern: Shakeel would straighten up immediately and she would return home, but within weeks his rage would boil over, burning her.

Hasina Begum made a decision for Tahira: "You have to divorce him." She not only delivered the message for Tahira but gave her an exit plan, a room in her haveli. Shakeel didn't let go so easily—he insisted he would be the one to divorce Tahira, making her wait. But Tahira had escaped. Not even a kilometre away from Shakeel, Hasina Begum's high walls, social status, and most vitally, her unending kindness, ensconced Tahira in safety. In a way, it was the most secure Tahira had felt since she was a child, protected

8. A formal message/dispatch.

by someone who truly understood what it meant to be alone.

Tahira let her siblings in Karachi know she had a change of address, although she wasn't ready to deliver the news of her marriage ending yet. She received a reply from her ever-loving sister Zubaida, relaying that their brother Salahuddin was sick and had been admitted to the hospital. After nearly a decade away, Tahira would have to return to Karachi. And while her chest tightened as she thought of returning to the city, the last stanzas of Faiz's bittersweet poem gave her comfort:

Abhi charaag-e-sar-e-raah ko kuch khabar hi nahin
Abhi garaani-e-shab mein kami nahin aayi
Najaat-e-deedaa-o-dil ki ghadi nahin aayi
Chale chalo ki woh manzil abhi nahin aayihe

Streetlamp at the edge of the road has no notion yet
The weight of the night hasn't lifted yet
The moment for the emancipation of the eyes and the
  heart hasn't come yet
Let's go on, we haven't reached the destination yet

Chapter 11

MISSING DAUGHTERS

WITH OUR TRIP TO Haroonabad behind us, my parents and I left the strange military compound in Bahawalpur on a Wednesday morning. Three hours later, we were in a taxi from the Karachi airport back to my aunt Lubna's, thrust back into the chaos of the city. Midday traffic's symphony of horns was on full blast with black pick-up trucks carrying armed men in the back, silver Suzuki hatchbacks, and hand-painted rickshaws cutting each other off to race to the next red light.

Our driver, a man in his fifties with a dark moustache and lightly tinted, square-framed glasses, kept asking us for directions until my dad asked him why he didn't have a smartphone. Our driver explained he had been robbed by a man on a motorcycle while at a stoplight. My dad then asked him why he spoke to a stranger on the street, shuttling me back to many childhood conversations: What did *you* do wrong for this bad thing to happen to you? Despite—or perhaps because of—the invasiveness of his questions, observing my dad speak to strangers made me think he would have been a good journalist. I found it mortifying when I was younger, the way he'd say hello to cashiers in Cantonese or Arabic, ask where they were from, when they came to Canada, how long they'd been running their stores. It turns out this kind of behaviour was exactly what I needed to emulate to succeed in my chosen career: being annoyingly curious and unselfconscious enough to ask deeply personal questions is a surprisingly large part of my job.

The driver, unfazed by my dad's rudeness, told us a man knocked on his window, and while he never rolled it down on the street, he noticed there were two women on the back of the bike. The man then pulled a gun on him, and our driver valued his life more than his wallet or phone, so he handed them over and hadn't been able to afford another smartphone since. "I thought he just needed directions," he said mournfully. "I didn't imagine he would rob me when he was with women."

While I felt for him, I thought about how clever it was for those women to use their perceived lack of power to their advantage. Powerlessness is conflated with innocence, and there's a sweet irony in using it as cover. Even in retelling the story, the driver assumed the women were just along for the ride. I'm not an advocate of pulling guns on people, but it was the result of a set of calculations made by these women about how to take advantage of their disadvantages. It made me think about a certain calculation Daadi made that I learned about in Haroonabad.

In Haroonabad, I learned while Daadi told those closest
to her she had four sons, she never mentioned her three
daughters. My stomach dropped when I first heard this
and I started thinking through why she would have done
this. Hasina Begum was a widow with five sons—for
Daadi, talking about her four sons was a way to cultivate
closeness with her. And of course, in a deeply patriarchal
society, having boys conferred a certain status. There's also
the shock of sheer numbers—leaving four children behind
sounds less reprehensible than seven. And the fact that they
were young girls, between the ages of six and nine, deemed
powerless and in need of protection during those tender
years, definitely made Daadi a less sympathetic figure.

I saw many instances of Daadi acting out her internalized misogyny as a child—the way she treated my mother,
primarily—but this was the most unsettling. And if she
erased her daughters because having only sons would
elevate her in others' eyes somehow, did that mean she
believed that notion herself, or was she just reacting to the
culture around her?

If my mother had pretended I didn't exist, the reason
she did it wouldn't change the pain I'd feel as a result of
that decision. I wanted to tell my dad's sisters about this
erasure before they read about it, but I didn't know how to
relay what would surely be a painful blow. As a journalist,
my training and experience is in interviewing people to
build trust in order to have meaningful conversations. I've
developed a sense for knowing when to push a little harder
and when to back off. As a result, people tell me difficult

things all the time. But I don't usually have to relay that information back to the people it would hurt the most.

When we got back to Lubna Phupi's place, Bushra Phupi was bustling around the house—figuring out last-minute visits to her in-laws, packing then weighing her suitcases. She was visiting from a city just outside Toronto, where she had lived since the early 1990s. Standing at five foot nothing with large hazel eyes and a sweet smile, she had a delicate beauty to her. When I was a child, she was equal parts loving and slightly terrifying, a strict mom to her three girls, and ready to call out any child on their foolish behaviour. She mellowed as she aged, but she was still as fiercely loving as ever. It was Bushra Phupi, after all, who noticed how harsh Daadi was with me and my sister in her complaints about us when we were kids and asked her to be kinder to us. "If you show children love, they show you love back," she told her mother. "But if you don't love them, they won't love you back."

Bushra Phupi sat with me for a bit, and I told her what we found in Haroonabad briefly. Although I hemmed and hawed about it, I blurted out that Daadi might have told some people she only had sons. Bushra Phupi was quiet, and then got up to finish her packing. I instantly regretted telling her. I don't know why I rushed it—maybe I felt so uncomfortable with the knowledge that I wanted to pass it on. I realized that I had made a faulty assumption: when someone has been through a lot, it can be tempting to think they're better able to absorb difficult information. But it actually means they should be treated with extra care.

MY CONVERSATION WITH BUSHRA Phupi threw me into uncertainty about whether I should continue to chase the last big interview I hoped to get on the trip: Shakeel's daughter.

The last time I was in Pakistan, Lubna Phupi had told me that when she was at a wedding, a family friend brought over a woman named Saba, who was a few years older than her. Lubna Phupi realized who she was and held it together enough to say salaam and politely move on. But since then, my dad had been trying to figure out how to get in touch with her. Our trip to Bahawalpur helped us in this long-running mission—my dad met a distant relative of Saba's and finally got her number.

The day after our return from Haroonabad, my dad pushed me to call her. The investigative bug had bitten him—he had been both shocked and thrilled we found so many people who knew Daadi in Haroonabad, and he now itched for more information.

It was late morning, and the heat had started to set in when Lubna Phupi and I congregated in the room my parents were staying in to discuss the merits of calling Saba. I knew very little about her—who her mother was, whether Shakeel left her mother or if he was a widower, and whether she was even raised by her father. It was one thing to ask my family to speak with me, to give them time to process and decide to participate in this intimate investigation, and another to call a stranger and ask about a potentially traumatic period of their life.

On the one hand, this was the *only* person I found who

could help me create a more nuanced portrait of Shakeel, who so far seemed like an abusive bully who enjoyed poetry. On the other, I might reopen deep wounds for an elderly woman who thought this part of her history was long behind her. But I went back to some good advice a senior reporter gave me at the beginning of my career: You have the right to ask, and they have the right to say no.

The three of them sat on the cream bedspread dotted with burgundy flowers—my mom leaning against the headboard, legs outstretched, Lubna Phupi perched on the right side of the bed, my dad sitting behind his sister while I paced at the foot of the bed. Lubna Phupi dialed the number, and as Saba answered, the rest of us gathered closer to listen to one end of the conversation: "I'm Khala Tahira's daughter, Lubna. How are you doing ... I was sad to hear about the death of your husband ..." It went on like this for another minute and then she got to business.

"There's something I need from you," Lubna Phupi started. "Tahira's granddaughter is here from Canada and she's writing a book about her. She's been to Bahawalpur and Haroonabad, she's met with people, taken photos and recorded interviews, and she's hoping to meet with you. And how are your kids?"

I looked at my dad after the bizarre pivot, as Lubna Phupi nodded her head and murmured "hmm" repeatedly in response to however Saba's children were doing. She seemed to be employing the secret Pakistani strategy of persuasion—a combination of small talk and misdirection that I will never understand, let alone master.

She then started talking about the wedding they met at. A bit of silence, and then: "Those eras are gone, those people are gone, what's left?" My dad stood up at this point, losing his patience, revealing that after nearly fifty years in Canada he was in fact more Canadian than Pakistani. "Get her address," he muttered.

Lubna Phupi got back on track, extracting that Saba lived in Gulistan-e-Johar. She then thrust the phone into my hand for me to say salaam. I heard Saba's voice—soft but clear, tinged with the texture that deepens with age. We set an appointment for the following week. "It brought me great happiness to speak with you, Sadiya," she said as we said goodbye, which could have just been a nicety, but they were words I couldn't have imagined she'd say before the call. I only noticed after we hung up that while Saba had mentioned Daadi many times, she hadn't mentioned her father once.

IN THE DAYS LEADING up to the interview, my dad kept asking me if I had my questions ready for Saba. This was annoying for several reasons, but mostly because my dad often assumed I was disorganized—despite me pulling off the trip to Haroonabad, in a country he grew up in, without his assistance. I also didn't want this part of my work to be under scrutiny yet. I was doubting my abilities enough as it was, and I didn't need his running commentary on my methods. But I also knew in many ways this was a team effort: the Western notions of owning a story and telling it the way you want to tell it simply didn't, couldn't apply here.

We headed out early that Tuesday evening, questions in hand, instructed to come between asr and maghrib, directions doled out in the fashion that those wedded to prayer times tend to provide. We said salaam to the chowkidar and entered a parking lot surrounded by aging white apartment buildings.

Saba's flat was on the second floor, and she greeted us at the door. She had a slight stoop, warm brown eyes framed by prominently arched grey brows and a sweet smile. Her hair was covered by a grey cotton dupatta, matching her shalwar kurta, which had intermittent bursts of delicate rose and violet star-shaped embroidery.

The living room was off the entrance to the flat, lined with alternating armchairs and loveseats, all in the same velvety grey and white printed fabric, worn thin where bums and arms rested over decades. I wondered if Shakeel had ever sat on these very seats.

I sat perched on the coffee table in front of Saba to be able to hold my mic, my dad behind me on an armchair. Her daughter joined us, sitting on the side of the room closest to the hallway, making our set-up feel like we were performing onstage.

I was hoping Saba would have a photo of Shakeel. He was always described the same way—tall, thin, with thick black-framed glasses, appearing to be at least a decade older than Daadi. Saba told me that she had some photos and a copy of his passport until very recently, but she came home one day to her son and daughter burning them all, deciding it was haraam to have photos in the house.

This extreme interpretation of the Quran is a symptom of the puritanical form of Islam increasingly practised across the country. Luckily, the resistance to media didn't extend to recording audio. We started recording minutes after entering the flat, and Saba was totally comfortable with the mic, proudly telling me she was a radio host in her university years.

It turned out the little we knew about Shakeel's backstory was incorrect. He wasn't a decade older than Daadi, but five or six years older than her. And he wasn't from Haroonabad as we first assumed. He was from Ambehta, Daadi's ancestral home in northern India. He went to Aligarh University in Uttar Pradesh, also in northern India, and was part of the All-India Muslim League—the political party that ultimately agitated for a separate Muslim state. Shakeel moved to Pakistan in 1948, with his wife, Aqsa, when Saba was just six months old. While his wife had deeper roots in Pakistan—her family had moved to Quetta decades before Partition—Shakeel didn't have many connections. That's how he ended up in such a small town—it was the only place he could land a decent job as a municipal clerk.

Shakeel would accompany Aqsa on trips to Quetta, sometimes leaving her there to spend time with her family. On one such trip in the winter of 1956, Aqsa took Saba so the young girl could spend time with her naani. One night, Aqsa decided with her sisters to wake up early, before fajr, to eat sehri and fast, but when her brother woke up for fajr, he noticed no one else was up yet. So he called out to Aqsa, and heard her reciting the kalima. "He called out to her and she kept reading the kalima," Saba told us. "So he kept calling her, and then she became quiet."

After that, Aqsa's mother woke up, and as she walked by her daughter's feet, she noticed they were stiff. That was when her family discovered Aqsa had died that morning. She was twenty-six.

Aqsa's family stepped in to take care of Saba—they lived in a multigenerational household with her parents, siblings, and their children. For them, it was just taking care of one more of their own, while Shakeel didn't have anyone else to lean on in Haroonabad. He came to see Saba every six months, but after a few years, the period between visits stretched into a year.

We had been chatting for about half an hour when she told us this, and my dad piped up with a question. "Your father didn't support you, and he ignored you," he said, shaking his head slightly in an agitated manner. "Why did you stay in touch with him?"

Saba calmly explained she never felt ignored by her father. But he pressed on. "Don't mind my question," he said. "How was your relationship with your father given he almost abandoned you?"

I felt mortified, and tried to defuse the situation, although it was a perfectly relevant question and I was grateful I didn't have to ask it myself. I was still finding it a bit disorienting to just walk into someone's home and ask about the most intimate details of their life—yes, that was my actual job, but the cultural taboo was so ingrained in me that doing so with my family present, in Karachi no less, was uncomfortable. But later I realized my father was talking to a peer—someone he thought he had a lot in common with, someone he thought might have felt as abandoned as he did. When listening to the audio from the interview again, I thought about the hurt he might have felt in that moment when you realize someone doesn't feel the particular pain you thought you shared.

When the gaps between Shakeel's visits to Quetta stretched to four years in 1967, Saba went to visit her father. She was attending a wedding in Bahawalpur with her uncle, and they decided to take the train into Haroonabad to stay at her father's home for three days. She was charmed at the sight of the town's older buildings—in Quetta, the 1935 earthquake that killed thirty-five thousand razed the city, and it was rebuilt in the monotonous style of a British cantonment town. She arrived at her father's two-room home, meeting Daadi for the first time, who immediately started cooking for her guests.

Saba and her uncle sat in the kitchen while Daadi minced garlic and ginger, chopped eggplant and tomatoes, and told the stories behind her unlucky marriages: her first, a forced marriage to her phupa, her second prompting a boycott from her children. Daadi said her stepchildren told her she couldn't meet with any of her children, and that she missed them very much. She then read Saba a poem she wrote for her children—Saba still remembered the first line: "Nazar se nazar thak baray fasley hain." The young woman's heart sunk when listening to her stepmother evoke a vast distance with her words.

After Saba returned to Quetta, Daadi wrote her a letter asking Saba to live with them in Haroonabad. But Saba was still in school and couldn't imagine trading the family who raised her for another one. She still wrote to her father, but didn't see him for another three years—at her wedding in Quetta, where he arrived alone. By that time, Daadi and Shakeel had divorced.

Dad jumped in at the mention of the divorce with a question that sounded more like a statement. "I heard your father was an angry man," he said.

"Yes, he could be angry," Saba responded, nodding in acknowledgement. "But it was the kind of anger that came quickly and cooled quickly."

My father wasn't satisfied with the response. He sat through people telling him Daadi left Shakeel because of his abuse—her neighbours from fifty years ago still had visceral memories of his voice reverberating through their shared wall. "But I heard—and please forgive me for being so candid—that he disturbed your mother so much, she got tuberculosis and died as a result."

The absolute last place I wanted to be then was sitting on a coffee table passing the mic back and forth between those two. Of course, the question didn't make any medical sense, but what he was trying to get at was something we both had been told second-hand: that Shakeel's first wife's death had something to do with him wearing down her spirit. Saba refuted it, taking us through the circumstances of her mother's passing again.

Though Saba was a bit younger than my father, she had

the air of a big sister. She spoke in measured sentences
and imparted larger lessons through her recollections. She
was never impatient with the nature of his questions and
wasn't afraid to push back when she felt something wasn't
characterized correctly. And she was fair toward Daadi.
She spoke respectfully of her, and was quick to point out
how young Daadi was when she got married: How much
could someone who experienced that be blamed for the
choices she made later?

And she was generous toward her father, in life and in
death. While he stayed in Haroonabad for another twenty
or so years after the divorce, he would visit Karachi, bringing carrot halwa for his grandchildren and local ghee for
Saba to cook with. Saba offered to put him up when he
finally retired and wanted to move to Karachi. That was in
1988, and what they didn't know then was they would spend
only six months together. Shakeel became sick suddenly,
dying after a short hospital stay.

As we wrapped up, I asked my dad if there was anything
else he wanted to know. "This is a critical question," he
started, leaning in so I could capture his voice on the mic.
"Did my mother ever tell you what happened when she
married Shakeel sahib, whether she left by her own volition,
or if Shahab told her to leave?"

Saba didn't know. But she did have some wisdom for him:
"You weren't necessarily told the story as it happened—
when someone tells a story, they tell it in their favour."

The agitation I saw in my father earlier in the conversation returned, and this time it felt like it came from a

different place: finding it difficult to accept there were some things we wouldn't be able to uncover. "This was the question I never got to ask her," my dad told her.

"Let me tell you one thing, she was your mother," Saba said. "There are many things our elders kept to themselves. They were not all sahaba, they were regular people who made mistakes."

Chapter 12

KINSHIP

AS TAHIRA HELPED HASINA Begum raise her children, a woman named Hasina Khatoon ended up raising Tahira's.

After Tahira left, aunties—by blood and by proximity—checked in on her children for the first eight months until their father's only sibling came to live with them. Phupi Amma, as her nieces and nephews called her, joined them from Dhaka after recovering from a nasty fall, no small thing at the age of seventy-four.

Hasina Khatoon didn't have children of her own—she gave birth to one child who died at four years old. After much heartbreak, she adopted a daughter, Aqueel, with her husband, Mohtashim, a poet who lived off inherited wealth. Mohtashim had an unfortunate penchant for taking new wives, secretly marrying a woman named Qamar Ara Begum shortly after the adoption, without telling either woman she would be one of two wives. Hasina Khatoon was able to reconcile with him over this, finding relative peace in a joint household.

His next secret marriage came years later, but was completely unforgivable. When Mohtashim decided to marry Aqueel, in one fell swoop Hasina lost her daughter and her husband. Disgusted by him, she wrote to Ehsan. He came to collect her, witnessing his brother-in-law's doleful attempt to make his first wife stay—laying his topi at her feet, asking for forgiveness. She left that day, and never saw him again.

Returning to Hyderabad, she assumed responsibility for Ehsan's seven children after their mother died in childbirth. And thirty years later, she left her adopted city of Dhaka to raise his younger lot. Arriving in Karachi, she tried to conceal her shock at the condition of the home, the condition of the children. The older brothers had tried their best, but the younger ones had a wild look in their eyes from months of neglect.

Immediately, Hasina saw what they needed: good meals, a schedule of sorts, and most importantly, tenderness. She bought hoards of seasonal fruit at cut-rate prices—oranges in the winter, mangos in the summer. She would take extra effort to cook on the weekends, when their older brother Zia often visited, making shami kebab or Hyderabadi khatti daal. She had a stock of achaar year-round that she made herself from pickled turnips, mangos, and lime. Her real expertise, though, was in sweets, especially homemade laddoo.

Hasina Khatoon tried to instill deen into the children,

who had little religious guidance after their mother left. She'd tell them well-worn religious stories to lull them to sleep: Adam's descent to earth, Nooh's chaotic ark, Ibrahim's unthinkable sacrifice. They were familiar lessons, ones she imparted to her own brother as a child, after they lost their mother when he was just seven and she became his third parent in a way at eighteen. Even when Ehsan was an adult, married with children, she'd advise him when she thought it was vital. She remembered when he came to her to seek counsel about the tension between his second wife and Tahira. Using her own experience to seal the wisdom of an old adage, she delivered three lines to her brother:

> *My friend, do not engage two mates at a time*
> *As you will lose your shirt and pants to one,*
> *And your moustache to the other.*

SEVEN YEARS AFTER TAHIRA left Karachi, she returned with Wajahat in tow, staying with her ill brother's wife, Sabiha, at their home in Hyderabad Colony. Salahuddin was the softer of her brothers, accepting of Tahira even after her second marriage. His wife made up for his soft edges with her chatpat Hyderabadi speech and her tendency to make every dish sour. Tahira's youngest brother, Rashid, also balanced Salahuddin. When he arrived at his brother's home to support Sabiha, he was surprised to see Tahira and was terse with her at first. But to her relief, Rashid warmed a bit with each meeting.

Tahira would go to the hospital daily with Sabiha to visit Salahuddin, then head home to cook in an effort to ease her sister-in-law's burdens. After three weeks of this routine, Salahuddin was released. Relief flooded Tahira when she realized that she wouldn't have to watch her younger brother be buried.

With Salahuddin home, surrounded by his children, Tahira's attention drifted to her own, less than a thirty-minute drive north from Salahuddin's home. How would she explain that she left the man she left them for? That her great sacrifice was worth nothing but more pain? She wasn't ready for that. She needed time to figure out what she would be asking of them—forgiveness? To move back in? The chance to be their mother again?

As she watched seven-year-old Wajahat play in the court-yard, it was decided. Tahira would return to Haroonabad without visiting her own children. She couldn't turn up with Wajahat at 3F. How could she explain she had been helping raise someone else's children?

THE FIRST FEW YEARS Tahira was at Hasina Begum's, she took over managing household affairs—doling out tasks to servants, going shopping at the market, even cooking at times, since Hasina Begum hadn't managed to step into the kitchen since her husband died.

Tahira stayed on the main floor, in the family's most intimate quarters. Rooms lined one side of the courtyard, separated by a wooden screen, called a jaali. The haveli was a multi-storey home, common in South Asia, dividing large homes into areas for men and women. This was to accommodate purdah, creating a large space for women where they could live, cook, and raise their children without being seen or heard by men outside the family whom their husbands might entertain. Open-air spaces like courtyards and terraces helped with airflow, especially in the hot summer months. While colonial eyes often saw the structures as oppressive, they provided privacy for women like Hasina Begum, who chose to stay ensconced in her haveli long after her husband died.

The courtyard also acted as a barrier between visitors and gharwallay.[9] The stairs going up from the sehen revealed a large terrace and more bedrooms. These rooms would be filled when the boys started to get married as their wives moved in and their eventual progeny filled the floor with sounds of laughter and tears. But Tahira ended up moving upstairs before any of Hasina Begum's children, since her two eldest sons were still away at school.

After Tahira settled into a rhythm in the household, her older sister, Zubaida, turned up with their younger sister, Saleha, and her son Irfan. They had written to Tahira, and she invited them to Haroonabad, but was slightly nervous about proposing Zubaida stay on. Hasina Begum didn't blink—there was plenty of room, and so she offered them space to stay. Saleha returned to Karachi, but she sent Irfan back to Haroonabad, knowing he'd get more attention and

9. People who live in the home.

education in Tahira's care. Hasina Begum moved the three of them into a room upstairs, and Tahira didn't feel this was too much of an imposition since Farhat and Shujaat were both away at university. But once Farhat returned home and Tahira organized his wedding arrangements, she knew her days at the haveli were numbered.

To prepare for this eventuality, Tahira asked Hasina Begum to use her connections with local authorities to get her a job at the government's school for girls in town. At first Hasina Begum refused—she didn't need more income coming in, and she was happy to take care of Tahira. When people assumed Tahira was her sister, she didn't correct them. In her eyes, she was. Tahira had been there for her during the most difficult decade of her life.

Hasina Begum's refusal touched Tahira, but she knew the haveli was getting crowded, and Hasina's boys were grown now—Hasina didn't need her the same way she once did. Tahira was stubborn, bringing up the matter until Hasina finally relented and helped her get the job. Tahira then acquired a new routine, setting off every morning with her neighbour Safiya, who also taught at the school. The pair would walk down winding dusty alleys, arriving at a metal gate painted cerulean blue, set between two brick pillars painted pale pink. Rising from the pillars was a sign written in Urdu script but with English words: MC Girls Primary School, Muhajir Colony. The chowkidar would nod at them politely, opening the gate to an open-air play area lined with garden beds, leading to the covered portion of the school where the principal's office and few classrooms sat.

Tahira loved teaching. It was her chance to be respected, to be an authority. Other than Safiya, the teachers were all at least two decades younger than her; they not only looked up to her as an elder but thought her to be worldly with all the cities she had lived in, her way with poetry, her talent in telling a story. Tahira could spin an ordinary occurrence into a serial, and on the rare occasion something dramatic actually happened in their small town, they'd be rapt hearing her retell it.

One particular morning when Safiya set off earlier than she did, Tahira walked to the school alone. She was pulling her abaya beyond her wrists when she was interrupted by a young man's voice behind her. "What time is it?" he asked, smiling slyly, in an attempt to convince her to push her sleeve up a few inches to reveal her wrist. Tahira was hot with anger—after years of living in a woman-run household, teaching at a woman-run all-girls school, she didn't have patience for this young man who decided to try it on with her, unable to see her face even, not knowing she was old enough to be his mother. Without thinking, she slapped him across his left cheek, hurrying away before he could recover from the shock. Fear left her as she passed the entrance into the school, taking off her abaya and relaying the story to her colleagues drinking chai. Students lined up outside the gates, waiting to be let in, slightly confused as their teachers' laughter carried out of the school, nearly drowning out the bell.

Tahira remained close with Safiya as her friend became principal, finally confiding in her that she couldn't keep living at Hasina Begum's. Zubaida and Irfan were still with her, and wedding preparations for yet another one of Hasina Begum's boys meant one more person would be moving into the haveli. Safiya's rise through the ranks meant she had a bit of room to manoeuvre at the school. There was a classroom next to her office that was seldom used since lessons were mostly conducted in the courtyard. The square chamber was no more than four metres on each side, with a low ceiling and no windows—a far cry from the room that opened up onto a terrace that Tahira currently enjoyed. But Safiya offered it to her friend—it was all she could provide within her power.

Tahira felt at ease when she moved herself, her sister, and her nephew into the room. There was a water pump just outside, an indoor washroom, and she was able to build a makeshift stove in the smaller courtyard just off her room. It took her back to those early days at 3F with no electricity—she had managed then and she would manage now. Tahira still saw Hasina frequently, and while she missed their symbiosis it felt good to no longer feel dependent on anyone, even another woman.

As an Islamic studies teacher, Tahira was, like most religious figures, strict and slightly terrifying, not just to students but also to her younger colleagues. Tahira didn't mean to scare the girls—they were in primary school after all, the oldest among them only ten years old. She just wanted them to know the difference between right and wrong, to resist the temptations life would throw at them and choose the straight path even when lying or cheating would be so much easier. Tahira wanted the girls to know they couldn't afford to make mistakes: there would be no second chances for them, not here and not in the afterlife.

But sometimes she would pretend she didn't see her favourite student passing a note to her classmate, a glint in her eye giving away her attempt to suppress a smile. On those days, she would recite a dua for them, praying that their friendship would last, so when mistakes were inevitably made they would have one another to turn to.

Chapter 13

GOLD

WHILE MARRIAGE IS THE ultimate gateway to security in my culture, and some, like Daadi, were lucky enough to have a network of women to rely on when that failed them, for centuries there has been one other thing South Asian women could fall back on: gold.

The first time I wore my very own "set" was at my cousin Maria's wedding when I was fourteen years old. The choker was made up of a dozen gold medallions the size of dimes, with a yellow-flecked brown star stone in the centre of each one. The earrings replicated the coin pattern with a string of smaller gold disks that hooked into my hair, and the set was completed by a ring with a large stone set in the middle. The jewellery accompanied a rust-coloured gharara, each step I took swooshing the satin fabric of the wide-legged design. Wearing it all together felt like an initiation into womanhood.

My mother bought that particular set on a trip to Karachi. She visited every two or three years, taking pains to save money between trips, spending it on gems and precious metals that sat in a bank locker most of the time. The jewellery being collected would be formally passed down when I got married. Marriage and gold are inextricably linked across South Asian cultures and religions—it can act as both a dowry and financial security for a young wife. Your marital status also determines how much gold you can wear. Younger, unmarried women typically wear lighter chains, mirroring what widows wear on the other side of marriage.

What happens to the zaiver set aside for you if you don't get married? Comparing my experience with my sister's, the same thing happens: your mother holds all your jewellery for you in her bank locker. And that's consistent with cultural norms—you don't have to get married to inherit gold. A daughter has rights over her mother's jewellery, although a wedding marks an occasion where new sets are created for you.

While visiting my parents from Berlin in the fall of 2022, I was itching to buy myself a gold medallion to hang on one of the many chains I assumed I owned. But before buying something new, I thought I should check on what I already had, wrapped carefully in tissue paper, tucked into an institutional metal drawer a few kilometres from my parents' home. Surely there was something my mother put away for me that I'd want to wear. And surely there was something I was so certain I wouldn't wear that I could melt down and make into a simple ring that I could slip on every day.

On a crisp fall morning, my dad and I were planning to go to the mall, where the bank was. (My dad is a devoted mall walker, walking three kilometres a day for the last thirty years, rain or shine, arthritic flares or not.) Ammi put my name on the bank locker a few years earlier, wanting someone else to have access to it in case something happened to her. But I didn't remember how to access it, and I didn't have a key. When I asked her, her reaction surprised me: she refused to let me see the jewellery without her present.

And that *upset* me. Visiting my parents as an adult often triggers over-the-top meltdowns usually only seen by parents of hormonal teenagers, the kind I didn't actually have when I was a teen. I stormed out of the house, raging to my father in the car, "What was the point of putting my name on the locker if she doesn't even trust me to look at what's mine?" My dad was quiet for the first part of the drive, true to his annoying habit of not responding when someone is too emotional for his liking. But before we entered the mall, he informed me that he'd never had access to the locker, and he hadn't even seen its contents.

WHAT WAS IN THE locker was the domain of women—emeralds, rubies, pearls, diamonds, and, of course, gold. It is one of the few financial domains my mom alone could make decisions in, despite her being the savvier investor between my parents. A headline in the *Indian Times* declared that in 2020, Indian women owned 11 percent of the gold worldwide—this didn't surprise me in the least. The figure itself is hard to verify, but it's widely understood that the "demand and hoarding" of gold is a pan-Indian phenomenon that is "unparalleled," anthropologist Nilika Mehrortra writes. Gold holds many meanings—it symbolizes prosperity, feminine beauty, fertility—but the most important is social security for a woman. It is "the most acceptable and legitimate form of property women possess in the patriarchal set up."

In conversation with Mehrorta, she explained to me that a patrilineal inheritance structure meant men inherited land and women inherited gold. It was assumed women would get married, so they weren't given immoveable property—gold is easy to transport and is seen to be as liquid as cash. Not only is gold given to women as inheritance, and gifted especially during weddings, it's seen as a good investment. Everyone—from women like my mother returning to Pakistan every few years, to women from fishing villages in southern India with little expendable income—will save to invest in gold.

Before bank lockers were accessible to the middle class, people would hide gold at home, digging holes underneath the stove. Historically, gold saved families during hard times. Mehrorta has seen this in her own family's history. After her grandmother moved from Lahore to the Indian part of Punjab following Partition, jewellery was the only asset she had left. She sold it all, save for a pair of earrings and a ring, to set up a new life.

Mehrorta herself refused the gold her mother wanted

to give her on her wedding day, telling her mother she was a feminist and didn't believe in a dowry. But after spending some time studying the significance of the fine metal, she realized the importance of handing it down. Not passing it on was like disinheriting your daughter.

TWO WEEKS AFTER MY initial attempt to survey my zaiver situation, my mother took me to the bank herself. The teller was a brown woman in her twenties, with long black waves and a yellow-gold necklace hanging around her neck, a tell-tale sign she knew exactly what kind of booty was in the long, narrow box she retrieved for us. We went into one of the two rooms reserved for this task, tiny with a desk and chair, with cobalt blue walls and a lock on the door. Ammi had meticulously organized what was mine, my sister's, and hers, and what she planned to pass down to her nieces and their children. As she carefully unwrapped each set, she told me where it came from—the familiar star stone one, the pearl one she was gifted by my dad's family when she got married, and an emerald one she made for me, the last of which was the only one she considered selling when times were hard.

Ammi showed me a gold ring her mother had given my father and told me I could have it remade into whatever I'd like. My naani had also given my father a gold watch, one my sister had copped a decade earlier that I was still incredibly envious of. But I couldn't bear to melt this piece down. I had spent so little time with my naani—she lived in Karachi my whole life and died at sixty-seven, when I was ten years old. There wasn't much I had left of her, in an heirloom I could touch or in my memory. I wanted to hold on to every tiny thing.

There were many other pieces Naani gave my mother, some which Ammi had already put aside for me. But the most meaningful gift was the one she gave Ammi before my mother headed to the airport to start a new life in Canada: three gold coins.

The difference between gold coins and other coins is that the actual gold is what's valuable about the coin—modern coins are about 92 percent gold. Countries produce their own versions, and while an American Eagle one-ounce gold coin has a denomination of fifty dollars, it's actually worth forty times that based on the weight of the gold. While gold bars are usually part of a bank's gold reserve, coins can make it into the mix, and if you take a gold coin to a bank, you can walk out with cash.

Naani knew all of this when she passed the coins into her daughter's hands and said: "Beta, dekho wahan takleef nahin uthana." She told her daughter if things became difficult, she could take these coins to a bank, cash them, buy a plane ticket, and come home. It was the least Naani could do to assuage her daughter's fears. After all, when my mother boarded her flight from Karachi to New York, she hadn't even met her husband yet.

"It was so painful, Sadiya," Ammi told me as she recalled the memory. Her voice was low but steady, then she paused and repeated herself in an even quieter voice: "It was so painful."

MY PARENTS HAVE TWO anniversaries—one is September 11 and the other is April 15. They rarely celebrated, and on their twenty-fifth anniversary, we had a very muted gathering since it happened to fall one year after 9/11. Even for a marriage arranged across two continents, theirs was especially unusual.

During Ramzan in 1977, my father's older brother Shams and his wife, Sajeda, approached Naani for my mother's hand in marriage. Shams was a close family friend, and Ammi's eldest sister and her husband pushed the marriage, insisting Rafi was from a good family.

When I asked my mother whether she was asked about the decision, she paused for a moment. Ammi said this was the first time she realized that no one talked to her directly about it. And she certainly wasn't asked. Ammi discovered her marriage had been arranged by overhearing her family speaking about her wedding with one another. Her words alternated from tumbling out of her to being punctuated by silences as she extracted these long-buried scenes from her mind. Her tone was inflected with a bit of disbelief, as if she was talking about someone else's life, relating the circumstances, and then commenting on them with the lens she has acquired with time: "That sounds really strange."

The wedding was rushed. Shams said they wanted the nikah done before Ramzan was over to speed up the immigration process. He told my mother's family Rafi would arrive for the rukhsati,[10] and after a tearful goodbye to her family, they'd leave for Canada together. A wedding during

10. The end of the wedding, when the bride is saying goodbye to her family of origin and being "given" to her husband's family.

Ramzan was odd—it was the holiest month of the year, and the multiday celebration nuptials required were usually put off until afterwards. But since my father's family was just asking for the nikah to be done over the phone, Naani agreed, which is how my parents' marriage was solemnized, underwater cables carrying their acceptances, their *kabul hai*, across twelve thousand kilometres.

Waiflike with delicate features, my mother sat in her mother's home in her red wedding lehenga, her dupatta draped loosely over her dark brown hair pulled into a braid, the gold-fringe embroidery hanging framing her face. Shortly after, she had her first phone call with my father. They wrote each other letters, my mother getting her friends to help her write hers—she was a math and statistics grad, not a student of poetry. And while Ammi's family patiently waited for my father to land in Karachi to have a proper wedding celebration, eager to meet the man they promised their daughter and sister to, they never imagined he wouldn't get on a plane to finalize his marriage.

What they didn't know at the time was that, like Ammi, my father also wasn't consulted on the subject of his own marriage. And just like Ammi, he only saw a photo of his new spouse weeks after the nikah, when it landed in his mailbox inside an envelope stamped airmail.

The reason his marriage was arranged with such speed was that he had asked permission to propose to someone else. Homesick and lonely after a few years in Canada, my father developed a regular correspondence with a family friend. He decided to tell his eldest sister he wanted to marry his pen pal.

There was immediate displeasure with his choice, and a plan was hatched to redirect his intention to marry to someone more suitable: my mother. He received the news by telegram a few weeks later: "NIKAH FIXED SUNDAY 6 PM PAKISTAN TIME." The short message was followed by a phone number, signed Shams. He didn't even know my mother's name.

"I thought it was a joke," my father tells me forty-five years later.

But his elder siblings were the closest thing he had to parents—he was expected to make the call, so he did.

My parents' nikah being performed over the phone became a funny anecdote I dined out on, an extension of the cultural tendency to see marriage in practical terms, in this case simply an administrative detail in an immigration application. But the reality was this hasty arrangement that was someone's idea of what was good for them changed the course of both their futures. And neither party was consulted on what their opinion was about it.

As terrible as this circumstance was for my father, it didn't help that someone in his family told Ammi the real reason behind the rush right after the nikah. When my mother was then asked to meet him in Canada, Naani was upset, and the elders in the family were outraged. But the nikah was already done. In the eyes of God, they were married.

AFTER NAANI GAVE MY mother the gold coins, she steeled herself to say goodbye, refusing to go to the airport with the rest of the family. Finally, after much convincing, she relented under one condition, turning to her daughter to extract a promise: "You will not cry at the airport."

Ammi nodded, and miraculously, kept her promise as she held each sibling close, saying goodbye. But as soon as she exited the doors past security, she broke down. Sitting in the lounge, her new reality set in: she had to make this long journey alone, to live with someone she had never met in her life. Putting on a brave face for her family intensified the fear that then overwhelmed her—it flooded her, her tears unable to escape as quickly as she needed them to, her body shuddering with the effort, her throat erupting with hiccups as she tried to breathe through it. Airline staff checked on her, asking her if everything was okay. What could she say?

On the insufferably long plane ride from Karachi to New York, she tried to cry quietly, but a flight attendant noticed and kept checking in. As the plane nearly reached the unknown continent she'd soon call home, Ammi changed into a shalwar suit her mother had ironed and placed carefully in a garment bag so her daughter could make a sharp first impression. It had some light embroidery, signalling that her tears weren't prompted by a death but an event normally considered a celebration. When the flight attendant noticed, she asked Ammi if she just got married. She nodded, and the attendant asked if she could do Ammi's makeup. She sat beside my mother, carefully running a mascara brush over her lashes, livening her cheeks with blush.

As my mother told me all of this over the phone one night, I was grateful I wasn't sitting across from her. And as it happened, that evening FaceTime just wouldn't cooperate, so we settled to do the interview over the phone. I stifled my sobs so she wouldn't hear, picturing my young, sensitive mother, who loved the countryside and her siblings more than anything else in the world, alone on that plane, flying farther from both.

I ASKED AMMI IF she ever thought about using the coins. She immediately said no. She had two younger unmarried sisters, and everyone would have blamed her older sister, who arranged the marriage, for it breaking down. And there was something about her mother's rare instance of softness in handing those coins to her that made her even more determined to make it work. When I asked if she regrets not using them, she said no, but the reasons were all still rooted in what was best for her family, not what was best for her.

Through confronting Daadi's past, I have been trying to unlearn the myth that earlier generations were simply more resilient. But I also had to face that this was true for my mother's generation as well. That generation of women formed the connective tissue between Daadi's and mine—a bridge across an impossible divide. Daadi lived in a world where she rarely spoke with men outside her family, and as a woman in her thirties, she was expected to kill any desire of her own after her husband died. Ammi was a woman who grew up in strict purdah, transported on Bannu's streets by a carriage driver who wasn't allowed to look at her and her sisters as they climbed in. Ammi didn't even like moving to Karachi—it was too busy for her. I grew up thinking I would likely live in my parents' home until it was time to move to my husband's.

I see the push and pull in my mother: an intuitive woman who understands the freedom I need as her child but is afraid of it. Afraid of what will happen to me as a woman alone in the world, afraid of what people will think of me. When I moved to Germany, my mom told me she wished she had the opportunity to do what I did—explore by choice. I was exasperated by this response. It made me feel immensely guilty for all the opportunities she didn't have. I wanted her to just be happy for me, and I didn't realize then it was perhaps the highest compliment she could have given me, naming her own desire and commending me for accomplishing it.

I sometimes wonder what the twenty-four-year-old Shahnaz would have done if she had the freedom I have—before she became a wife, before she became my mother. I think of her in my favourite photo of her from early in her marriage: long hair cascading over a salt-and-pepper wool coat tied at the waist, her hands in her pockets, wearing slouchy calf-high black boots while looking out into the horizon.

THERE WAS A SINGLE piece of jewellery sitting in my mother's bank locker I was sure I would never wear: an intricate, star-patterned pendant on an eighty-centimetre gold chain. Daadi passed it down to me. The pendant was massive—I had never worn it and was never going to wear it. Like many South Asian women of my generation, I wear gold but in a more subtle way. And in that sense, it was the perfect piece to remake into a simple ring, a way to carry Daadi with me without looking like Mr. T. But my mother refused. "She loved this pendant," Ammi said.

Teenage rage rose in me again. I didn't understand how honouring Daadi's gift meant keeping it locked away and never making use of it. But what I have realized since is that my mother wasn't just trying to preserve a superfluous adornment.

Not only was the pendant a symbol of security, it was also an inheritance. There easily could have been a version of Daadi's story where she wouldn't have known me, let alone handed down gold to me. It wasn't just a privilege for me to receive it, it was a privilege for Daadi to pass it down to me. An opportunity she didn't always have with her own daughters.

Chapter 14

REUNIONS

WHILE TAHIRA'S CHILDREN HAD a vague idea of
where she was, she kept closer tabs on them. Her siblings
would deliver news surreptitiously, without revealing to
their nephews and nieces how close they still were with
their mother. That's how she learned Shahab had left for
Toronto, followed by Razi; that her sister-in-law, who was
caring for them, had died; and that Lubna was the first
of her children to be married. And when she found out
Bushra was set to follow, Tahira managed to coordinate a
trip to Karachi, hoping she'd find the courage not to miss
another milestone.

Staying with Salahuddin, Tahira decided since she made
the journey across the country, she could make it across town
to go to the banquet hall. Venues like these had multiplied
as Karachi's population continued to grow exponentially in
the decade she had been gone, becoming the economic and
cultural centre of the country. It was also a frequent stop

on the "hippie trail," much to the chagrin of conservatives who were tired of seeing hippies' pasty bodies on the beach. But they were in the minority. Westerners seeking "authentic" living were such a boon to the local economy that the government launched a tourism ministry in the early 1970s. Tahira didn't approve of the cinemas that seemed to be on every corner, or the bars and nightclubs cropping up, but there was a fullness the city had acquired that reminded her of Hyderabad—a living thing rather than the sterile plots of land in Nazimabad allotted to muhajirs when the first wave landed twenty-five years earlier.

After arriving at the venue for Bushra's wedding, Tahira stood outside for a moment, taking in the twinkling lights. She felt her heart cramp as she recognized those she used to call her family—women lining one side of the entrance to the hall, and men the other, rose petals ready in hand to shower the groom's family with in welcome. The groom came into view, his family surrounding him, waiting to time their entrance just right. Through the chatter, she was able to pick out a woman's voice asking where the mother of the bride was. Tahira perked up until she heard another woman solemnly respond that both of Bushra's parents were dead.

Tahira took one last look at those familiar faces eagerly waiting to greet this new branch of family and wondered which one created this story, which ones repeated it. It was one thing to be cast out of her family. It was another to be pronounced dead. Tahira went straight back to her brother's home, which lay quiet and empty until he and his family returned from the wedding.

ALTHOUGH BUSHRA'S WEDDING WASN'T the return to her family she had hoped for, six months after the event, Tahira found that the kind family her daughter married into would be in her favour. Eager to see Bushra after her wedding, Tahira enlisted her cousin Asho's help to make it happen. Asho called Bushra at her new home in Nazimabad, just a ten-minute drive from her own, asking if Asho could come pick her up and bring her over to her home. Bushra naturally asked why, but Asho was coy, just telling her she had a surprise for her.

When Bushra walked into Asho's home, a woman was sitting in between two of her mother's cousins. Asho asked Bushra: "Don't you recognize her?" Bushra had no idea who the woman was. "It's your mother," Asho said excitedly.

They had a brief visit during which Tahira had a difficult time containing her emotions. This was in sharp contrast to Bushra, who felt nothing. She was nineteen years old, and her mother had been gone for over a decade. She had few memories of her, and as a result, little remaining attachment.

A few days later, Asho arrived with Tahira at Bushra's new home unannounced. It was a multigenerational home, her husband's siblings and father all living under one roof. And while Bushra had told her husband that her mother was alive, her in-laws still believed she was dead. The lie that her eldest siblings told her new family to simplify their past and shield them from scandal had only landed Bushra in a far more awkward situation.

When Bushra's father-in-law learned Tahira was in fact

alive, he was dismayed to hear how she had become an outcast. He invited her for dinner to try and normalize relations. But Bushra was still uncertain about her own feelings as she navigated her new role in her husband's family and at a tender time in her own life, early in her first pregnancy, about to become a mother herself. As the evening went on, polite conversation gave way to laughter, and while Tahira wasn't able to win Bushra over as a mother, there was a cautious warmth between them.

This dinner gave Tahira the courage to reconnect with Lubna two years later, and Lubna's husband, Jawed, proved to be especially welcoming. Tahira had been waiting for one of her sons to bring her back to the family, but it was her daughters who created a bridge. By acquiring new families, they acquired new permissions, new perspectives.

WHILE HER DAUGHTERS PROVIDED the bridge, hope of formally returning to the family lay in being invited to live with one of her sons. It was Jawed who took Tahira's youngest son aside and told him she was visiting Karachi. "She needs you," he told Shamim.

That was in 1978, and by then, Shamim's older brothers had all departed for Canada. He was still single and living with Shams, one of his many older siblings from Ehsan's first marriage who supported their younger ones through their tumultuous childhoods. Shams was an exceptionally loving brother into Shamim's adulthood: providing him space in his home to live, teaching him to drive on his fleet of hobby cars, getting him a job right out of school. Shamim knew seeing his mother would upset this balance.

But Jawed's words sparked an urgency in Shamim, so he decided to meet his mother at Asho's house as a first step. It had been fifteen years since he had last seen her, and the woman who left him in her early forties was now in her late fifties. She didn't quite look elderly yet—her long hair was still black, her laugh still forceful. But Shamim noticed she seemed coated in a weariness.

After an evening of careful conversation—catching her up on his studies and what he hoped to do as a textile engineer—Tahira suddenly began crying uncontrollably. Shamim moved to console her with a hug, and after they embraced, she stayed close, holding his shoulders as her eyes moved across his face. As she saw how his features had sharpened, how her young teen had become a man, the years she missed became painfully real.

Shamim moved quickly to ease this pain: he asked Tahira to quit her job in Haroonabad and move back to Karachi to live with him. She hesitated at first, asking him to think about it. She was particularly worried about what it might mean for his relationship with his older siblings. She knew they had a hand in raising him. It wasn't fair to make him choose. But Shamim was less concerned. He respected his elder siblings deeply, but he didn't want his mother to suffer in isolation any longer. He soon persuaded her: "As your son, it's my responsibility."

They said goodbye, this time certain they'd see one another again. As Tahira went to wrap up her affairs in

Haroonabad, Shamim started looking at flats for rent, knowing that bringing her to Shams's house was out of the question. Within a few days he signed a lease for a modest flat in Yousuf Plaza, on a busy throughfare. He waited until the lease was finalized to tell his brother he was moving out and braced for his anger. But it was Shams's sudden indifference that struck Shamim as he hobbled under the weight of his luggage on the way to the door. Shams, usually so eager to help, ignored him completely.

TAHIRA RETURNED TO MUHAJIR Colony Girls' School, carefully preparing the final lessons she would teach her students. Teaching had given her a sense of purpose separate from the other parts of her life; a sense of duty, a sense of value. On that final November morning at the school, she taught her students the meaning of Surah Al-Maidah, which, among other things, speaks to Muslims' relationship with "People of the Book"—Christians and Jews. One line stood out: "Do not let the hatred of a people who once barred you from the Sacred Mosque provoke you to transgress."

It was a lesson for both Tahira and her students, and part of what she loved about teaching was becoming more learned herself. At the end of that day, Tahira opened the notebook she recorded each lesson in, the beige and grey snakeskin cover giving way to lined paper inside, and wrote: "*School ki kardagi / Meri umer bhar ki poonji.*" It had been her life's work. And despite leaving it—and all the people who helped her survive—behind, for the first time in her life she prepared for a move she chose with her whole heart.

WHILE TAHIRA'S RETURN MENDED one rift, it created another. Other than Rafi and Zia, Shamim's older brothers refused to speak with him. But he didn't quite understand how strongly they felt until Shahab's wedding in Karachi, when Shamim realized his older siblings had gone ahead with yet another marriage repeating the myth of being orphans. But he attended the valima, the last in a string of wedding events, at his mother's insistence.

He spent that evening, and many others, floating between conversations, feeling like an outsider among those he had spent his whole life with. At another family event, his mood finally took a turn after Razi's father-in-law approached him. "Ah, so you're the one who brought your mother home," he said, patting Shamim on the back. Shamim hadn't realized how much he needed someone to affirm his decision.

That small kindness moved Shamim to focus on what he gained rather than what he lost. After all, his mother's return taught him there was always time to repair relations. And those first days of having a mother again were some of the brightest of his life.

THE TASK OF RUNNING her own household again energized Tahira, and as the weeks and months went by, she started to shed her air of weariness. She fell into an easy rhythm with Shamim—choosing tchotchkes so the flat was warm and welcoming, shopping for groceries, and planning elaborate dinner menus for when Shamim's friends would visit. She still had the companionship of Zubaida and her nephew Irfan, who joined her in her new life. The rest of Tahira's family came over often, and one of her stepsons, Zia, and his wife, Zohra, honoured her return by dining with them every Saturday.

This reunion planted hope that more were possible, and slowly, as Shamim's siblings started speaking with him again, this hope grew.

There was one event that would cement Tahira's place in the family again: a wedding. After two years of living with Shamim, she decided to become proactive about her sole unmarried child's betrothal. Not only did Tahira want to attend his wedding, she wanted to arrange it herself. She found his future wife's family, set up a meeting, then a proposal, then the wedding. She used the money she had saved over the years from teaching to buy his future wife, Saima, a gold set, and persuaded her brother to call on a contact he had at one of the most desirable shaadi lawns in the city.

The event brought together nearly all Shamim's siblings and provided an opportunity for Tahira to meet her children who had left for Canada. Rafi returned to Pakistan for the wedding for the first time since leaving the country. He and Tahira met under the watchful eye of his eldest half-sisters, and she could see him trying to restrain his emotion out of respect for the women who had taken care of him when she hadn't. Tahira didn't hold it against Rafi—she took it as a sign he had been raised well.

A LITTLE OVER A decade after that meeting, Tahira sat on a pink velvet couch in Rafi's living room in a home outside Toronto. It was the beginning of April, and the sun began to warm her lap on this mild spring day. In the three years since she arrived in Canada, her idea of warmth had transformed. The temperatures that marked the darkest days of winter in rural Punjab now marked a pleasant day, a promise of sunnier days to come. It was Shahab who brought her to Canada in a reconciliatory act she hadn't imagined possible. In his renewed filial devotion, her oldest son sponsored her immigration, as he had done for many of his siblings.

But moving to Toronto hadn't been as smooth as returning to Karachi. After a few years of trying to fit into Shahab's household, she moved in with Rafi, sharing a room with his youngest daughter. Tahira tried to slip into her role as family matriarch, her strong personality bolstered by this renewed status. Her children were always polite, listening patiently to her advice on how to best cook bhindi or the fastest method to sew a shalwar. But Tahira knew she couldn't really be their mother again, not in the way she wanted.

Still, on occasions like this crisp April morning, Tahira was given the reverence she craved. It was the first day in a month the household didn't rise before dawn to prepare for the fast ahead. Instead, she woke to the smell of roasting pistachios that would top the sheer khurma served warm from the stove, the delicate vermicelli noodles softened in a sweet milky broth.

The dish never tasted quite like it did back home, but it became part of a new ritual. After breakfast, her children would soon file into the house after mid-morning Eid prayers. They spent their mornings ironing out the creases from clothes shipped from Pakistan, wearing the gold at the back of the drawer, sprinkling saffron in desserts for the special occasion. Her visitors would ensure they hugged her first—three times as was tradition—and then track down the inevitable runaway child who had wriggled away to swipe a pakora from the table, pulling them by the arm while nagging, "Did you say salaam to Daadi?" They would all gather around the table, piling samosas, slow-cooked eggplant, and chicken biryani on their plates, ladling the still-warm sheer khurma into small bowls. Her children would dole out two-dollar bills to their nieces and nephews, the young ones then scurrying off to sit on the stairs and count their loot.

Although she could never have a truly fresh start with her children, it was these grandchildren who gave her the gift of a new beginning. Her children didn't forget her past, but they kept her secrets.

Chapter 15

RESTING PLACE

ON A TRIP BACK to Berlin from London, I emerged from the SBahn station on a miserable January evening, dragging my metallic grey carry-on across cobblestones, telling myself in ten minutes' time I'd be warming up in my flat. I felt a light rain, but when I looked up, saw it was wet snow. Fat, half-melted flakes fell onto my navy coat, and I stopped to stare at a streetlight illuminating the magic of it all. I just told a friend earlier that day that I missed snow. The endless grey of Berlin winters had me feeling like I needed a way out before the next season of darkness fell—it was the lack of sun I minded, not the cold. The white blanket brightening the streets felt like home.

In one generation, snow became entwined in my family's DNA. We weren't mountain people—not from the part of the subcontinent where the Himalayas meet the sky. But every move, every displacement reconfigures what home feels like: my mother's tendency to be on German time, my father's insistence that Pakistani mangoes are objectively the best.

At different points of researching and writing this book, I became paralyzed thinking about how long life can be: where you can start and where you can end up. I would think about the ten overlapping years I had with Daadi, and what it meant for her life to be ending in the place where mine was just beginning. And what it meant that I only got to know her two decades after she died. I wondered if she ever missed snow on her rare visits back to Pakistan. Whether she still longed for the fresh milk from Ehsan Manzil, aam from the yard of 3F in Karachi, or the akhrot ka halwa from Punjab. I didn't have the answers to these questions, but through this process, I had at least acquired better questions. I transformed the two-dimensional brown grandmother I grew up with into a human with needs and desires akin to my own. I always saw the bold women in my family in her image—my sister, my cousins Shama and Aisha. But I came to see what I shared with Daadi: a love of words, a talent for writing, an unfortunate attraction to disappointing artist types, and most importantly, a pulsing desire for freedom.

THE GREATEST GIFT THAT came from immersing myself in Daadi's life was insight into one of my own parents. In a way, I could only really meet my father by knowing his mother. Before this inquiry, he too was mostly two-dimensional to me—a hard-working immigrant, an entitled brown man happy with the comfort gender roles of his generation afforded him. When I hit the red button on my tiny Sony audio recorder that first time in 2017, I didn't consider what I would learn about him: the small moments of joy in his childhood, the bigger disappointments he filed away, or the heavy trauma he carried with him with every move.

When I started, I didn't think much about what I would learn about my father. Daadi's story had this clear arc of hardship and redemption. I imagined it recast in a feminist light—a woman taking control of her life. But as I got further along in writing this, it became more difficult to give people the elevator pitch of what it was about. How do you compress displacement, loss, poverty, and forgiveness into a neat package? There was the shock of a woman of my grandmother's generation leaving her children and living on her own, in rural Punjab no less. But was that surprising because of the history it was rooted in, or did the Western gaze that rendered women like her powerless make it surprising? Was it simply that any act of agency of this exotic species became worthy of exploration, perhaps proving we did in fact share something with Western women?

I discovered Daadi was one of many women in my family who defied these simplistic narratives: Hasina Khatoon left her objectively terrible husband, my father's eldest sister, Razia, held her family together while her husband was wrongly jailed for years as a suspected Razakar, and many women never married at all. And they represent just a speck in the long history of women resisting what has been foisted on us. But that resistance ends up being cast using the same boring patriarchal tropes centring men in every decision: in Daadi's case, it was a selfish act to get remarried, and in Phupi Amma's case, leaving her husband was necessary to live a virtuous life. These stories rarely mentioned what these women *felt*.

And despite what they felt, women like my daadi held on to the suffocating myth of womanhood, instilling in their daughters and granddaughters there was one way to be good: to be faithful and obedient. I thought about this during a visit to the Tate Modern, where the first installation I was confronted with was titled *confess* by British Indian artist Bharti Kher. It was a chamber with dark wood panels that made up four walls two-and-a-half by two-and-a-half metres high. Warmly lit by a bare bulb in the middle of the ceiling, it resembled a prison cell, but Kher has described it as a bridal chamber.

It reminded me of a chamber in Sunjeev Sahota's novel *China Room*, where teenage brides were sent on the nights their mother-in-law decided they should sleep with their husbands. The three young women didn't even know which brother they were married to, adhering to a purdah so severe they never saw who was entering them, only feeling their weight. The china room, already a prison of sorts, lives up to its cruel potential for one of these brides when it becomes the chamber fifteen-year-old Mehar is trapped in for years after she's tricked into having an affair with the wrong brother, one she thought was her husband. Kher's chamber has a lock on the outside, much like Mehar's.

But in Kher's chamber, there's a beautiful world inside. Its walls are covered in colourful bindis that, she once told the *Times of India*, have been "recording the secret confessions of the woman who resides in the room." And all that gets translated on the outside is shadows from the cut-out patterns bordering the top of each wall that provide ventilation—wooden bars in one row, hollowed stars below them. The shadows are a reminder that keeping women shut in isn't without consequence for those on the outside, and the vibrant walls inside prove a woman's ability to have a rich inner life no matter the venue.

There's a false binary of the type of woman you can be—one who can settle into the role of victim comfortably and one who resists it by refusing to enter the chamber or breaking out. I think about the binary my extended family imposed on me early in life: my sister was the pretty one, I was the smart one. This limited us both. It set me up to grow in opposition to my sister, set her up as dangerous because of her beauty, set me up as responsible because of my mind, my aqal. These types of binaries steal complexity from us, steal reality from us.

The traditional story of the good girl who complies and the bad girl who rebels has been turned on its head in modern pop culture—the former is the dullard upholding patriarchy, while the latter is the heroine we've been waiting for, the one we hope to become. But every woman resists what doesn't feel good, in small and big ways. And those who haven't been able to leave their chambers sometimes raise a generation who will—that's not always the fluke we think it is.

But rebellion is not always a feminist act. Rebellion is not always an admirable act. We aren't individualized atoms solely responsible for our own choices as much as Western culture would like us to believe. Choosing yourself as a woman has consequences that can't be glossed over in a neat narrative arc. Daadi was a woman who both left her children and longed for them. A woman who had circumstances imposed on her that damaged her greatly, and who made choices that may have damaged her even more. Choosing a man wasn't a feminist act declaring her freedom: it was a desperate attempt to carve out a tiny slice of life that could be her own, yoking herself to yet another person whose desires would come before hers.

When I first became curious about Daadi's story, I wondered if motherhood was something she wanted. But it became clear that life without her children was torturous for her, not exactly the definition of freedom any of us would seek. Celebrating her separation from them as a feminist act of sorts was simply incorrect. A feminist act would have been her extended family making room for her desires—women cannot do that on their own. Often, the most feminist acts must be committed by men. If the antidote to shame is empathy, as Brené Brown puts it, shame is the patriarchal punishment, while empathy is the feminist act.

HAVING SUCH A LARGE extended family that didn't, in theory, differentiate between full siblings and half-siblings made for an interesting childhood. But there was an oppressive element in having such a sprawling family tree—the feeling that I was being surveilled by dozens of people. What I wore, how I spoke, who I said salaam to first. I had to leave my city, again and again, to snip that tether—both so they couldn't see what I was doing and to learn not to care if they did. It made feel like a bit of an outcast, and I was surprised when a younger cousin told me she admired my independence as she was finding her own. I became so accustomed to making excuses for the way I lived that I didn't realize it could be admired. And I shared with her what it took me years to realize: Coming from a big family is complicated, and having to be a certain way to be accepted by people is difficult and sometimes painful. We all have different paths, and we all deserve to be loved by our families even if those paths are not quite what they imagined for us.

Unexpectedly, writing this book has strengthened my sense of belonging to my family, as I am. It's a bit sad that their love and affection surprised me, that even in my generation, I felt love was conditional on following a familiar script. My family went above and beyond in their trust and openness with me during this process. And it dawned on me that of course they had the ability to stretch for the ones they loved—their hearts were big enough to embrace their mother again. This wasn't a fairy tale where all the loose connections were somehow restored. It was a deliberate act to be exceedingly kind, generous, and forgiving.

Every family has loose connections, lost connections,

and cords that have been cut. But growing up as an immigrant in the "new world," looking back is often a selective
exercise, making it easier to pretend these complications
don't exist. The places we land are often built on these selective narratives: papering over difficult histories, recasting
genocide as a celebration of "discovery," for instance. And
the focus becomes continuing to build—new is better, leave
the past in the past. We buy new clothes, new cars, newly
built homes to fit into this new place. There's an obsession
with forward motion, with growth. But how can you grow
things on scorched earth? Soil depleted of minerals? In
joining me on this circuitous, and at many points, painful,
journey, my family gave the gift of enriching my soil. Giving
me a richer life, more room to grow.

And what I hoped to give them in return was a portrait
of the kind of woman who is often whispered about, but
never written about. I wanted Daadi to be remembered as
she was, not in a caricatured arc of failure and redemption.
After all, that's how she wanted to be remembered. After
she died, Shahab Chacha found a couplet written on the
back of a photo of her:

Khak main mil jayai ga jub mairi hastee ka nishan,
Yadgar-e zeest hogi taza iss tasweer saiy.

When all signs of my existence turn into dust,
Memories of my life will bloom afresh from this photo.

IF I ACHIEVED NOTHING else, there is one small moment that made this inquiry worthwhile. A few days after returning to Karachi from Haroonabad, my dad and I sat with Lubna Phupi for dinner. The three of us had settled into a routine of doing our own thing during the day, and meeting at the dining table for meals Lubna Phupi lovingly made for us, rising every morning at six before the gas was turned off to ensure we had fresh kebab or pulao that day.

We were sitting chit-chatting about everything from where to buy the best bedsheets to the latest political crisis, when my dad suddenly piped up with a question.

"Do you think Daadi can see in heaven that we made this trip?" he asked, looking up at his sister. Lubna Phupi nodded vigorously.

"And do you think it made her happy?" he asked, hopefully.

"Yes, of course," she responded.

The comfort that washed over my father's face is a sight I'll never forget.

Tahira in her room in Rafi's home in
Markham, Ontario, 1998

TRAUMA REVISITED

"THESE ARE THE MEMORIES I don't want to recall, but you're asking."

That's what Shahab Chacha said to me right after telling me about the conversation he had with Daadi the day she left them. I was sitting in my apartment in Toronto, perched on a stool, my laptop and recorder in front of me on the kitchen counter, his voice coming through my iPhone speaker. It was in 2017, shortly after I did my first set of interviews with my dad. When I reached out to my uncle, he was so friendly and eager to speak, setting up a time immediately, opening the conversation by asking how my job was going. But the tone shifted after about a half hour. He didn't object to any of my questions, but after answering them, it became clear he would have preferred not to.

I have learned over time that when I ask people questions as a journalist, they feel they must answer. It's a strange power dynamic—I could be asking a question in the most tentative way, but the interviewee feels they *owe* me an answer simply because they agreed to talk in the first place. I really only realized this when being interviewed myself. I try to be savvy, knowing a recorder is on, but sometimes I just *talk*. And I don't mean everything I say—speaking out loud is my process to digest things, come to conclusions. That's dangerous with a recorder on.

When I teach interviewing to budding journalists, I start off by laying out the type of expectations they should set out for "real people." It's a weird label, but I basically mean those who aren't media-trained experts who know how to give you a pithy soundbite, or politicians who regularly dodge answering a question. Most people don't know the role or rules of interviewing in journalism—that you can't just take something back weeks after you've disclosed it, or decide something is off-the-record after the fact.

When people express nervousness before an interview, I often tell them that they are in control of what they disclose: *If you're worried about telling me something, just don't tell me—take time to think about it. You can always tell me later.* I tell students to reject the received wisdom that the best kind of interview feels like a conversation. I don't want an interviewee to feel completely at ease. I want them to understand this is not like a conversation with someone they know and trust.

That's why it gets complicated when interviewing people who already trust me (you know, like family). Journalists are typically not permitted to interview friends and family because it complicates the relationship between interviewer and interviewee. But memoir is a different beast. And as a result, I've often been asked: *How do you interview your family?*

Before responding, I usually take a deep breath, trying to focus on the lessons I've learned and not the sizzle reel of mistakes that steal sleep from me. First, I tell them: *Interviewing those close to you is tricky—you risk not going far enough in an interview, or going way too far.*

I've become much more concerned about the latter, partly because I have a feeling that early in the process of researching this book, I pushed too hard. So I remind students that there's inherent risk in interviewing people who have implicit trust in you—they might not distinguish the conversation from any other one they'd have with you. I advise students to create theatre when sitting with those closest to them: place an audio recorder in their view, making it clear this is a different kind of conversation. Ask them to say and spell their name, give their date and place of birth, even if you know those things. Make them feel like they are onstage, that these words are being performed for an audience, even if their faces aren't visible yet.

I've generally been good at that part. But in almost every other respect, I have fallen down. Most notably, there are clear guidelines for interviewing people who have experienced trauma, but I wasn't taught these in school or advised about them by any editor I have worked with in my decade-long career. Luckily, these guidelines have become more mainstream in the last five years or so, and there are now ample resources available online.

Trauma comes in many forms. It's a normal emotional response to an abnormal event, as the American Psychological Association puts it, or series of events. It could be a singular event like an assault, or a pattern of behaviour, like being neglected as a child. The response to these kinds of experiences can vary from emotional to behavioural to cognitive. It can prompt confusion, sadness, anxiety, and numbness. It can trigger a survival response that affects memory—witnesses of a traumatic event may not be able to recall it accurately. The long-term impact of all this can be depression, anxiety, PTSD, and substance abuse.

One of my aunts often remarks that there have been no long-term effects on her siblings from the difficulties they went through, that they all built lives that far exceeded what anyone expected of them. Building a solid life is an incredible feat for those who had to climb out of poverty without parents, but it doesn't overwrite the experience of those hardships. And it doesn't mean there aren't lingering effects. I realized that this narrative of "success," in combination with the decades that had passed since they experienced their father's early death and their mother leaving, meant I didn't consider that I could trigger the feeling of powerlessness those events created.

Not only was this incredibly naive, but it was irresponsible. The most important part of interviewing people with trauma is ensuring the process doesn't make them feel retraumatized or revictimized. "Trauma robs the victim of a sense of power and control over her own life; therefore, the guiding principle of recovery is to restore power and control to the survivor," writes psychiatrist Judith L. Herman.

One of my aunts is chatty and a vivid storyteller. I had interviewed her before, and on one occasion, when she started talking about her childhood while we were both visiting Karachi, I asked her if I could record her. She immediately admonished me: "These were very traumatic events. I don't want to repeat them again and again." I tried to be more careful after that—realizing her storytelling abilities didn't shield her from the harm of reliving the feelings those memories bring up.

When people ask me about interviewing family now, I add that because the interviews will likely involve resurfacing difficult events, they should use the principles of trauma-informed interviewing—which has implications for before, during, and after an interview.

These protocols differ from those in a standard interview. And I've messed up just about every single one. Here are a few I've adapted from the Dart Centre for Journalism and Trauma and insightful pieces from trauma specialist and survivor Louise Godbold and reporter Alice Wilder.

Ensure they feel in control

Establish at the beginning of an interview that your interviewee can take breaks, choose not to answer questions, determine the pace, and end the interview whenever they want. I assumed the power dynamic between my parents, aunts, and uncles was clear—their cultural status as elders meant they held the power in every situation, every inter-action we had. Of course, they wouldn't answer questions they didn't want to. What I didn't consider early in my reporting was that the theatre of the recorder changed that dynamic. It's evident in Shahab Chacha's words about not wanting to recall events.

Give them what they need to be comfortable

"Would you say it slowly, I am hard of hearing," my dad's half-brother Zia said to me as we sat in his home just outside Seattle in the summer of 2018.

When I interviewed him, he was nearly ninety years old. I knew him only as someone who wore a hearing aid, and in his old age, his hearing had deteriorated even further. I had to speak into a tiny mic where the sound was ampli-fied through headphones for him to be able to understand the questions I was asking. The feedback was horrible and made me cringe, making me lower my voice—which wasn't helping anyone. Eventually, we worked out a system where I would type out questions on his iPad and he would answer them. Relistening to the interview, I didn't understand why I hadn't just started the interview that way. And then I realized I didn't want to embarrass him—but there was nothing to be embarrassed about. I would have made him more comfortable by acknowledging his difficulty rather than trying to make him power through it, all while asking him to recall decades-old events.

Avoid asking "How did you feel?"

I caught myself asking my father how he felt about his eldest brother immigrating to Canada three years after his mother left. "We didn't have any choice how to feel," he responded. I could tell he was agitated by his tone, so I left it there. (Relistening to my tape, I realized I wasn't always so perceptive.) Sure, it's a fascinating statement to mine, but what does it provide the reader if he did pinpoint an emotion? Anger, sadness, abandonment—these are sort of obvious. I don't need a quote from him; I need the reader to understand the gravity of the situation. Retelling the events does that, not soundbites naming a feeling. Asking "How did you feel?" is not often a high-yielding question, and honestly, it's like looking for trauma porn.

Don't ask more than one question at a time

When my father told me Shakeel just turned up one day and started living with them with little preamble, I was confused. Instead of processing it and then following up, I asked every question that entered my mind all at once: *Do you remember the first time you met him? Like, do you remember thinking, what is he doing here? Did anybody ask Tahira? Did she say anything? She never explained it? She just brought him home?*

Being asked more than one question at a time is over-whelming—which do you answer? And if you're recalling a traumatic event, being hit with query after query can feel like an interrogation.

If they are visibly upset or withdrawn, offer to take a break or stop the interview

Shortly after this, I can hear my dad slowing down on the tape. I can hear him fading thirty minutes into the interview as I'm getting more energized, pushing him for more information. "To be honest with you, I don't recall what happened fifty-four, fifty-five years ago."

I moved on to the next set of events I wanted to cover when I should have asked if he wanted to pause, maybe have a cup of tea, and turn the recorder off for a while. It might seem obvious to, well ... anyone, but it took this interaction for me to really understand that if my dad was having trouble remembering something, it wasn't helpful to keep pummelling him with questions. It never helped me understand something better, and it only irritated my dad. It's something I would have never done with someone I wasn't close with. And here's some wisdom I gained only in hindsight: the most fruitful memories came years after these first conversations, only after he started to reach back to that time, to speak to his siblings about it, and after he became more comfortable revisiting it. Patience rather than persistence would have helped in those earlier interviews.

INTERVIEWING PEOPLE FOR OVER a decade helped give me some of the confidence I needed to take on this investigation. But my training as a journalist left me ill-prepared for this type of interviewing. As a daily reporter, you're trying to get as many people on the phone as you can, get your quote, write your story, file, and maybe have time for dinner and a full night of sleep before you start again. You are trained to think you have one shot to get "it." Luckily, I've now spent most of my career out of news. And experience has led to trusting myself more, basically making me more human: slowing down, paying attention, acting with more care. Realizing that the risk isn't not getting "it"—the real risk is inflicting damage under the guise of just doing my job.

There's a valorized trait in the trope of the dogged reporter that can create this harm: she's driven by getting to the truth. Something that is verifiable by documents, photographs, multiple accounts. And she won't stop until she figures out what *really* happened.

But when talking to people about the most painful parts of their life, sometimes that kind of verification simply isn't possible—and the idea of uncovering an objective truth is pretty passé, even in journalism. My father and his siblings don't all remember the same events, even if they were all there, or they may remember them differently. I rarely interview two people at the same time, but sometimes I had no choice. I remembered why when interviewing two of my aunts on a hot July afternoon. They kept interrupting each other to make corrections, each memory recalled requiring a sidebar on whether it was accurate. I wondered if this was a live fact-checking process, or if new franken-memories were being created.

In all of this, I have found myself turning over a question

in my mind that's seemingly heretical for a journalist to ask: *What matters more—what actually happened or how someone remembers it?* After all, the latter determines how they feel about it, how they tell the story, how they've internalized its implications, and perhaps even how they live their lives.

AFTER SHAHAB CHACHA EXPRESSED the difficulty in speaking about his mother leaving, he turned the interview around on me: "What made you decide to write about Daadi?"

I gave him my honest answer at the time, which was my amazement at her ability to survive on her own and be accepted back into the family. While I acknowledged her independent life came at a great cost to her children, in relistening to the conversation, it comes off as a bit glib—a simple attempt to recast someone as a feminist heroine.

And then he shared a sentiment many of his siblings echoed since. "Whatever we discussed, the negative parts— that she left her kids for a man—I think it's something that should be kept out of the story," Shahab Chacha said. "People sometimes make mistakes, they make the wrong choices, but if you expose it now, I don't know if there could be a positive view on her life."

I explained that I thought that was the crux of the story. "I realized that she was a victim of a very conservative culture, that her whole life allowed her no choice, and I think that makes for a sympathetic person."

Shahab Chacha considered this but clearly disagreed,

pointing out her life was made harder by the choices she made. "A lot of things are better left unsaid," he said.

And then he pushed a bit further. "In your story, I would just put the positive points of her and leave this part out— how she left the children—because it will be not so pleasant for [us]," he said. "I know you are writing it from the heart, because you see she had a hard life and she was a survivor. I don't want to tell you what to do, but that's my suggestion."

It was a reasonable request, and one in which my uncle respected my agency in the process. And it was a request a few of his siblings had made—either echoing his desire that I focus on the positive, or expressing the desire to shield certain people from the negative, asking me not to share what I was working on with their spouses or daughters-in-law.

I wanted to acknowledge his discomfort but also be transparent that I asked those questions because that was what the story was about. Listening to the tape, I couldn't believe my resolve. Ironically, my facile ideas about the story gave me the strength to push forward. Later in the reporting it would have been more difficult to justify the story was worth writing about at the expense of his pain.

"It was a very traumatic experience for all of us," Shahab Chacha told me as we wrapped up the call. "We don't want to relive it."

SOMETIMES STORYTELLERS ARE GIVEN too much credit; sometimes we are just story takers. I didn't want to just regurgitate my family's history for the sake of good

content. I wanted to try and recast Daadi from villain into
human. But of course, her children had already been grap-
pling with this for decades. And being a witness to them
expressing thoughts they perhaps never had a venue to
share before was incredible. My father started question-
ing things out loud I'm sure he's thought about silently
for years: *Why did his father marry his mother? Why was
his mother punished for remarrying? Why did his generation
carry so much shame for something that shouldn't have been
considered perverse?*

I have often felt at the margins of my family, not having
done any of the things that were expected of me. But creating a space for us to speak about this long-buried past ended
up being such a gift for me to be able to connect with my
family on a deeper level than I imagined possible. However,
I'm still unsure whether I did more harm than good.

As I gathered these memories, there was part of me
that recognized what was good for the narrative—the
researcher using her editorial judgement. But in writing,
I became the descendant who was processing the realities
of her family's history. I was not listening to tall tales of
resilience, but having to make sense of all the details that
made them resilient. At times I would just be still, sitting
in front of my monitor, trying to understand what it would
feel like to see your mother pull away in a taxi and wait for
her return each day after. To be the mother waiting for her
son to forgive her.

After writing the chapter about Daadi leaving her children, I cried every night for two weeks. For all the time they

lost with her, for those we lost before they were able to speak openly about their pain, and for who I was about to lose. When writing about my father's last visit with Daadi, I was struck by a strange feeling: sadness for sure, but also awe. It was a realization of how much love there was between my dad and his mother. That he would take such a risk to see her, that she would take the little time they had together to just be with him, and not use it as time to try to strategize and fix things. There was such wisdom in how Daadi spent those moments.

Being able to deposit these memories and feelings deep in my bones through writing them persuaded me to keep going, and clarified why we ask people to revisit their trauma. There is a higher purpose in recalling the past as it was, not as we wished it was. It has explanatory power. But most importantly, it holds the possibility for that pain to be recognized. This happened and it mattered. It changed the course of at least eight lives. My greatest hope, which sounds so lofty I can barely type these words, is that recognition leads to healing. I think of my dad as a teen, his sisters as young children, being made fun of at school because their mother left. I think of them unable to speak to one another about her for decades. I think of Daadi writing unanswered letters to her children for years. And I hope this is where telling stories can help—for people to know we think about them, we feel for them, and we care about what happened to them.

ACKNOWLEDGEMENTS

I have to start by thanking the woman herself, Tahira Ishrat Ansari, and all those like her who coloured outside the lines and paid the price.

I have such deep gratitude to those whose memories and generosity were the building blocks for this story. My father's siblings: Lubna Jawed, Bushra Hasan, Humra Khan, Shamim Ansari and Shahab Ansari. Irfan Ansari, for sharing his memories of Haroonabad, and providing me with leads that were key to excavating Daadi's history in Haroonabad.

Razi Ansari, who passed away while I was researching this book, wrote an incredibly detailed memoir crucial for filling in details like what the veranda of Ehsan Manzil looked like. Mansoor Ansari, for compiling our family's history so meticulously, and answering my many questions. Ali Ansari, who sent me videos of childhood dawaats with Daadi.

Absolutely everyone else who was open to interviews. Special thanks to Rao Wajahat Ali Khan and Rao Shujaat Ali Khan for treating me like family. It's something that touched me deeply, and I'd like to think Daadi would be pleased to know we connected.

My mother's family in Karachi and Islamabad, who had front-row seats to the madness. Special thanks to Ahmed Bhai, who gifted me Manto's short stories and read embarrassingly early chapters, and years later, a draft.

For those who helped bring it out in the world: My agent, Samantha Haywood, thank you for the structural edits, strategy talks, and belief in my work. Thank you to my editor Shivaun Hearne for seeing the vision for this story and publisher Karen Brochu. Much appreciation for Michelle MacAleese, Jenny McWha, Melissa Shirley, and Emma Rhodes at Anansi, and copy editor Amber Riaz and proofreader Allegra Robinson. To my fact-checker Mashal Butt: I couldn't imagine anyone handling this more thoroughly, professionally and sensitively.

I was very fortunate to receive grants from the Canada Council for the Arts, Ontario Arts Council, Toronto Arts Council, and Berlin Senate Department for Culture and Social Cohesion. Writing a book like this required funds for travel and research, and a reprieve from the freelance grind. I simply couldn't have done it without this support.

And for those who supported me throughout the process of writing the thing:

Kelly Dignan for welcoming me with open arms in Berlin, being my rock when things blew up (repeatedly), and still managing to keep me on track. Your edits were thoughtful and kind, which is no surprise because that's so much of who you are as a person. You made me feel like a real writer.

Avneet Toor, Aisha Jamal, Sarah Ahmed, Kulsoom Ahmed, and Matthew Mpoke Bigg for being early readers. Jessica Wellman, who was so much more than an early reader, but pushed me to start, went through a million cover ideas with me and whose support helped me get to the finish line. Andreea Muscurel for the endless talks over tea and the gorgeous cover that puts Daadi at the centre of her own story.

My two Nic(h)oles: best co-workers, cheerleaders, and sleepover buds. Nichole Jankowski for all sorts of book-related support, from late night hand-holding to party planning. Nicole Schmidt for being an emergency-contact-level friend in Berlin. Natasha Grzincic, for being the woc mentor I needed. Carley Fortune for keeping birthday goals on track, writerly encouragement and assuring me I could write a "shitty first draft."

Saadia Muzaffar for being so generous with her time and translating letters—I couldn't ask for a better humnaam. Kiran Butt for helping with logistics in Haroonabad.

To friends who cheered me on, listened to me gripe, invited me on family vacations, and promoted my book aggressively before I was even finished: Mandy Yu, Simran Kang, Jaime-Anne White, Zi-Ann Lum, Katie Underwood, Akbar Khan, Soo Kim, Dafna Izenberg, and Amina Rai.

I've probably forgotten so many people who endured me during this period—I'm sorry and I love you.

Finally, my family.

Ammi, who taught me how to write before I was in kindergarten, somehow made time to take us to the library every week, and watched me wobble my way to finding freedom. I'm grateful for a mother who made me believe I'm her dil ka tokra.

My sister, Aliya, whose only complaint about the book was exposing how much older she is than me (I took it out in the end!!). You're the most brilliant, loving and fun sister I could ask for. On top of that you made Ariana and Sarina, my two favourite people in the whole wide world, the next generation of fearless girls I write for.

And most of all, I'm grateful for you, Abbu. You risked great pain in opening your heart to recall long-forgotten memories, and I can only hope solving a few mysteries along the way was worth it.

NOTES AND SOURCES

Introduction

Known as terminal lucidity: Jesse Bering, "One Last Goodbye: The Strange Case of Terminal Lucidity," *Scientific American*, November 25, 2014, blogs.scientificamerican.com/bering-in-mind/one-last-goodbye-the-strange-case-of-terminal-lucidity/; M. Nahm, et al., "Terminal Lucidity: A Review and a Case Collection," *Archives of Gerontology and Geriatrics* (2011), med.virginia.edu/perceptual-studies/wp-content/uploads/sites/360/2016/12/OTH25terminal-lucidity-AGG.pdf.

Chapter 1

I was finding joy: Amanda Ripley, "Complicating the Narratives," *The Whole Story* (blog), January 11, 2019, thewholestory.solutionsjournalism .org/complicating-the-narratives-b91ea06ddf63.

The second generation is trying: Elif Shafak, "Meet the Writers," interview by Georgina Godwin, *Monocle*, podcast, October 31, 2021, monocle.com/radio/shows/meet-the-writers/309.

"Remembering something": Jorge Just, "Memory Game: Did This Meal Really Happen?" *Every Little Thing*, podcast, May 2021, gimletmedia .com/shows/every-little-thing/v4hz6vz.

Chapter 2

That was the same year: Shadab Bano, "Wahid Jahan: a Reformer's Wife and Partner in Muslim Women's Reform at Aligarh," *Pakistan Journal of Women's Studies: Alam-e-Niswan* 25, no. 1 (June 2018).

Chapter 3

Pakistani American historian Ayesha Jalal: Ayesha Jalal, "The Legacy of Partition," *Dawn* (blog) and *Hindustan Times*, August 13, 2016, hindustantimes.com/static/partition/comment/the-legacy-of-partition-ayesha-jalal/.

Over the four years that followed Partition: According to an analysis of census data from 1931 to 1951, 17.9 million people migrated in the four years after Partition, but only 14.5 million were counted as migrants in India, Pakistan, and Bangladesh, leaving 3.4 million unaccounted for. Prashant Bharadwaj, Asim Khwaja, and Atif Mian, "The Big March: Migratory Flows after the Partition of India," *Economic and Political Weekly*, August 30, 2008, 39–49.

As the writer Saadat Hasan Manto put it: Maria Thomas, "Bombay Heart, Urdu Ink: A Guide to Reading Saadat Hasan Manto." *Quartz*, September 21, 2018. qz.com/india/1396544/mantos-urdu-writings-on-indias-partition-bombay-bollywood.

Chapter 6

In the British-controlled era: Key to my understanding of the subject of border controls post-Partition was an interview with Antara Dutta, lecturer in International Relations, Royal Holloway, University of London, and work by Haimanti Roy on post-Partition documentary identities. Haimanti Roy, "Paper Rights: The Emergence of Documentary Identities in Post-Colonial India, 1950–67," *South Asia: Journal of South Asian Studies* 39, no. 2 (2016): 329–49, doi.10.1 080/00856401.2016.1164022.

As they prepared to be moved: Saadat Hasan Manto, *Mottled Dawn: Fifty Sketches and Stories of Partition* (Delhi: Penguin Random House India, 2011), 7.

Hyderabad had been: My understanding of the makeup of Hyderabad post-Partition and ideas of citizenship were informed by Taylor C. Sherman's work, especially the idea that in this period "formal legal rules about who had the right to stay in India were less significant than ad hoc notions about who belonged in India." Taylor C. Sherman, "Migration, Citizenship and Belonging in Hyderabad (Deccan), 1946–1956," *Modern Asian Studies* 45, no. 1 (2011): 81–107.

Chapter 7

Chinese British writer and filmmaker Xiaolu Guo: "Notes on Love: A Conversation with Xiaolu Guo," public talk, daadgalerie, November 30, 2022, berliner-kuenstlerprogramm.de/en/events/notes-on-love-a-conversation-with-xiaolu-guo/.

"Stress can be used to motivate us": Anya Meyerowitz, "I Discovered That I Had Financial Trauma—Here's How I Overcame It," *Refinery29*, December 23, 2021, refinery29.com/en-gb/financial-money-trauma.

And a review of academic literature: Justine Gatt et al., "Trauma, Resilience, and Mental Health in Migrant and Non-Migrant Youth: An International Cross-Sectional Study across Six Countries," *Frontiers in Psychiatry* 10 (2019), doi.org/10.3389/fpsyt.2019.00997; Marshia Akbar and Valerie Preston, "Migration and Resilience: Exploring the Stock of Knowledge" (paper prepared for BMRC-IRMU, York University, May 2019), bmrc-irmu.info.yorku.ca/files/2020/06/Immigrants-and-Resilience-Working-Paper_Final_new7.pdf?x15611.

Chapter 8

Shamim knew she preferred: A key source in understanding the cultural significance of poetry in relation to Partition was Priya Satia, "Poets of Partition," *Tanqueed*, January 2016, tanqeed.org/2016/01/poets-of-partition/6/?preview=true.

Chapter 10

As she revisited: "Subh-e-Azadi: An Anguished Evocation of the Pain of Partition," Penguin Random House India, August 14, 2017, penguin.co.in/subh-e-azadi-an-anguished-evocation-of-the-pain-of-partition/.

Abhi charaag-e-sar-e-raah: Faiz Ahmed Faiz, *The Colours of My Heart: Selected Poems*, trans. Baran Farooqi (Delhi: Penguin Random House India, 2017).

Chapter 12

While colonial eyes often saw: A piece by Aysha Kaiser on looking at havelis through a feminist lens informed an alternative perspective on accommodation of purdah in these homes. "Deconstructing the Feminist Narrative behind the Haveli," *Brown History* (blog), December 22, 2022, brownhistory.substack.com/p/deconstructing-the-feminist-narrative.

Chapter 13

The figure itself is hard to verify: Nilika Mehrotra, "Gold and Gender in India: Some Observations from South Orissa," *Indian Anthropologist* 34, no. 1 (June 2004): 27–39.

Chapter 15

But in Kher's chamber: Neelam Raj, "Yes, I Am a Feminist," *Times of India*, May 20, 2010, timesofindia.indiatimes.com/life-style/spotlight/yes-i-am-a-feminist/articleshow/5731385.cms.

Afterword

"Trauma robs the victim": J. L. Herman, "Recovery from Psychological Trauma." *Psychiatry and Clinical Neurosciences* 52 (1998): S98–S103, doi.org/10.1046/j.1440-1819.1998.0520s5S145.x.

Here are a few I've adapted: Mark Brayne, comp. and ed., *Trauma and Journalism: A Guide for Journalists, Editors and Managers*, Dart Center for Journalism and Trauma, dartcenter.org/sites/default/ files/DCE_JournoTraumaHandbook.pdf; Louise Godbold, "Do No Harm: A Media Code of Conduct for Interviewing Trauma Survivors," *Pacific Standard*, August 1, 2019; Alice Wilder, "Trauma Informed Reporting," *Transom*, March 18, 2021, transom.org/2021/ trauma-informed-reporting/.

Additional Sources

Akbar, Syed. "£3.5 Million Hyderabad's Nizam Money Sent to UK, Karachi." *Times of India*, June 30, 2019. timesofindia.indiatimes.com/ city/hyderabad/3-5million-hyderabads-nizam-money-sent-to-uk-karachi/articleshow/70007503.cms.

Al Jazeera. "Mirza Ghalib: Legendary Poet of the Urdu Language." December 27, 2017. aljazeera.com/features/2017/12/27/mirza-ghalib-legendary-poet-of-the-urdu-language.

Alhmidi, Maan. "Educated Immigrants Face Underemployment as Canada Leads G7 in Educated Workforce." *Toronto Star*, November 30, 2022. thestar.com/news/canada/educated-immigrants-face-underemployment-as-canada-leads-g7-in-educated-workforce/ article_dceb2309-0ba0-5b66-a79d-7a271073e695.html.

Asian Human Rights Commission. "Women and Religious Minorities under the Hudood Laws in Pakistan." humanrights.asia/resources/ journals-magazines/article2/vol-03-no-03-june-2004/women-and-religious-minorities-under-the-hudood-laws-in-pakistan/.

Bahl, Vani. "Haveli: A Symphony of Art and Architecture." *New Indian Express*, October 27, 2014. newindianexpress.com/cities/ bengaluru/2014/oct/27/Haveli-%E2%80%94-A-Symphony-of-Art-and-Architecture-675871.html.

Batalova, Jeanne. "Top Statistics on Global Migration and Migrants." Migration Policy Institute, September 20, 2023. migrationpolicy.org/ article/top-statistics-global-migration-migrants.

Baumann, Andrea, and Mary Crea-Arsenio. "The Crisis in the Nursing Labour Market: Canadian Policy Perspectives." *Healthcare* 11, no. 13 (July 2023): 1954. ncbi.nlm.nih.gov/pmc/articles/PMC10340563/.

Bhalla, G. S. "Peasant Movement and Agrarian Change in India." *Social Scientist* 11, no. 8 (August 1983): 39–57.

Bhutto, Abdul Waheed. "Addressing Policy Gaps for Sustainable Coastal Management: A Way Forward for Pakistan's Coastal Ecosystem." *South Asia Journal*, July 16, 2023. southasiajournal.net/ addressing-policy-gaps-for-sustainable-coastal-management-a-way-forward-for-pakistans-coastal-ecosystem/.

Bollen, Christopher, and Julien Capmeil. 2021. "In the Berkshires, a New Generation Is Putting Down Roots." *Condé Nast Traveler*, May 20, 2021. cntraveler.com/story/in-the-berkshires-a-new-generation-is-putting-down-roots.

Brown, Brené. "Listening to Shame." Filmed March 16, 2012, in Long Beach, California. TED video. youtube.com/ watch?v=psN1DORYYVo.

Bumiller, Elizabeth. "Weekend Excursion: A Literary Tour of the Berkshires." *New York Times*, August 7, 1998. nytimes.com/1998/08/07/ books/weekend-excursion-a-literary-tour-of-the-berkshires.html.

Butt, Aamir. 2016. "Anarkali: Fact or Fiction?" *Nation*, March 18, 2016. nation.com.pk/18-Mar-2016/anarkali-fact-or-fiction.

Canadian Museum of Immigration at Pier 21. "Immigration Regulations, Order-in Council PC 1967-1616, 1967." pier21.ca/ research/immigration-history/immigration-regulations-order-in-council-pc-1967-1616-1967.

Carrick, Rob. 2022. "Comparing Toronto House Prices to the Early 1990s Crash." *Globe and Mail*, November 11, 2022. theglobeandmail .com/investing/personal-finance/household-finances/article-comparing-toronto-house-prices-1990s-crash/.

Center for Substance Abuse Treatment (US). "Understanding the Impact of Trauma." In *Trauma-Informed Care in Behavioral Health Services*. Treatment Improvement Protocol (TIP) Series, no. 57. Rockville, MD.: Substance Abuse and Mental Health Services Administration (US); 2014. ncbi.nlm.nih.gov/books/NBK207191/.

Chandran, Rina. "Smashed Bangles and No Red Sarees, India's Widows Face Colourless Life." Reuters, June 21, 2016. reuters.com/ article/india-widows-factbox-idINKCN0Z706V.

Chotrani, Ratna. "Azadi Ki Rail Gaadi: A History of Hyderabad Railway Station." *Siasat Daily*, July 21, 2022. siasat.com/azadi-ki-rail-gaadi-a-history-of-hyderabad-railway-station-2374340/.

Christies. "The Diamonds of Golconda." christies.com/en/stories/ india-legendary-diamonds-of-golconda-b778cf2a299945bc9fb6723 a10598b97.

Dalrymple, William. 2015. "The Bloody Legacy of Indian Partition." *New Yorker*, June 22, 2015. newyorker.com/magazine/2015/06/29/ the-great-divide-books-dalrymple.

Dalrymple, William, and Anita Anand. "Muhammad Ali Jinnah." *Empire* (podcast), episode 14. October 24, 2022. podcasts.apple.com/gb/ podcast/14-muhammad-ali-jinnah/id1639561921?i=1000583755176.

Dasgupta, Indraneel, and Diganta Mukherjee. "She Could or She Didn't? A Revisionist Analysis of the Failure of the Widow Remarriage Act of 1856." CREDIT Research Paper, no. 06/01. Centre for Research in Economic Development and International Trade, University of Nottingham. N.d. nottingham.ac.uk/credit/documents/papers/06-01.pdf.

Dawn. "Legend: Anarkali: Myth, Mystery, and History." February 11, 2012. dawn.com/news/694833/legend-anarkali-myth-mystery-and-history.

Doshi, Vidhi, and Nisar Mehdi. "70 Years Later, Survivors Recall the Horrors of India-Pakistan Partition." *Washington Post*, April 8, 2023. washingtonpost.com/world/asia-pacific/70-years-later-survivors-recall-the-horrors-of-india-pakistan-partition/2017/08/14/3b8c58e4-7de9-11e7-9026-4a0a64977c92_story.html.

Express Tribune. "Tomb of Anarkali: A Symbol of Resilience and Love." December 19, 2019. tribune.com.pk/story/2120724/tomb-anarkali-symbol-resilience-love.

Farooqi, Baran. 2017. "Between Patriotism, Partition and Pakistan: Here's How Faiz Ahmed Faiz Became a Poet." Scroll.In, June 13, 2017. scroll.in/article/840401/between-patriotism-partition-and-pakistan-heres-how-faiz-ahmed-faiz-became-a-poet.

Farooqui, Salma Ahmed. 2022. "And Quietly Flows the Musi (Musa) …" *Siasat Daily*, November 21, 2022. siasat.com/and-quietly-follows-the-musi-musa-2462545/.

Government of Canada. Immigration, Refugees, and Citizenship Canada. "Comprehensive Ranking System (CRS) Tool: Skilled Immigrants (Express Entry)." August 9, 2023. ircc.canada.ca/english/immigrate/skilled/crs-tool.asp.

Haddad, Mohammed, and Alia Chughtai. 2022. "Infographic: How Were India-Pakistan Partition Borders Drawn?" Al Jazeera, August 12, 2022. aljazeera.com/news/2022/8/12/infographic-how-were-the-india-pakistan-partition-borders-drawn.

Haider, Murtaza. "A License to Rape." *Dawn*, June 7, 2013. dawn.com/news/1016271/a-license-to-rape.

Hassan, Tanzeel. "Getting Women Their Due." *Dawn*, November 13, 2022. dawn.com/news/1720657.https://www.dawn.com/news/1720657.

Human Rights Watch. "Pakistan: Proposed Reforms to Hudood Laws Fall Short." September 6, 2006. hrw.org/news/2006/09/06/pakistan-proposed-reforms-hudood-laws-fall-short.

India Times. "Indian Women Hold 11% of the World's Gold" (video). N.d. indiatimes.com/videocafe/trace/indian-women-hold-more-gold-than-many-countries-568799.html.

Jayawardena, Kumari. Feminism and Nationalism in the Third World. London: Verso, 2016.

Kamal, Ajmal. "Sailing between Karachi and Bombay." Dawn, August 26, 2013. dawn.com/news/1038269.

Kaur, Navdip. "Violence and Migration: A Study of Killing in the Trains during the Partition of Punjab in 1947." Proceedings of the Indian History Congress 72 (2011): 947–54. jstor.org/stable/44146786.

Khan, Danish. "Jinnah Succeeded in Creating Pakistan but Failed at Another Onerous Task—Selling His Bombay House." Scroll.In, April 20, 2017. scroll.in/magazine/834176/jinnahs-house-in-mumbai-is-a-monument-to-the-frailty-of-human-beings.

Khan, Yasmin. The Great Partition: The Making of India and Pakistan. New Haven, CT: Yale University Press, 2017.

Krishnamurti, T. N. "Monsoon." Encyclopedia Britannica, December 2, 2023. britannica.com/science/Indian-monsoon.

Kudhail, Perisha. "Do Indian Women Own 11% of the World's Gold?" More or Less: Behind the Stats (podcast), November 4, 2023. BBC Sounds. bbc.co.uk/sounds/play/pogqlxy3.

Lamb, Sarah. White Saris and Sweet Mangoes: Aging, Gender, and Body in North India. Berkeley: University of California Press, 2000.

Lau, Martin. "Twenty-Five Years of Hudood Ordinances: A Review." Washington and Lee Law Review 64, no. 4 (2007). scholarlycommons.law.wlu.edu/wlulr/vol64/iss4/2.

Living Waters Museum. "Narratives of Change of River Musi in Hyderabad." livingwatersmuseum.org/narratives-of-change-of-river-musi-in-hyderabad.

Mahotsav, Amrit. "The Swadeshi Steam Navigation Company." Ministry of Culture, Government of India. N.d. amritmahotsav.nic .in/district-reopsitory-detail.htm?8445.

Mehmood, Asif. "Thousands Return to Wagah to Witness Parade Post COVID-19." *Express Tribune*, March 22, 2022. tribune.com.pk/ story/2349079/thousands-return-to-wagah-to-witness-parade-post-covid-19.

Mishra, Yuthika. "The Struggle Against Child Marriage: The Sarda Act (Act XIX) of 1929." *International Journal of Creative Research Thoughts* 1, no. 2 (September 2013). ijcrt.org/papers/IJCRT1134200 .pdf.

Moffelt, Miles, and Kristen Lombardi. "Ethics and Practice: Interviewing Victims." Dart Center for Journalism and Trauma, January 19, 2012. dartcenter.org/content/ethics-and-practice-interviewing-victims.

Munir, Sana. "The Lady behind the Sheesh Mahal." News International, June 23, 2019. thenews.com.pk/tns/detail/568004-101283.

Mustafa, Naheed. "Muhammad Iqbal: One of the Greatest South Asian Thinkers of the 20th Century." *Ideas*, CBC Radio, August 24, 2023. cbc.ca/radio/ideas/muhammad-iqbal-pakistan-founder-poet-philosopher-1.6725488.

Muthiah, S., and K. N. Gopalan. "The First Wheels Roll into India." Extract from *Moving India on Wheels: The Story of Ashok Leyland. Business Standard*, January 29, 2013. business-standard.com/article/ management/the-first-wheels-roll-into-india-108122301090_1.html.

Naqvi, Sibtain. "History: The City of Lost Dreams." *Dawn*, November 20, 2016. dawn.com/news/1297169.

Narasiah, K. R. A. "How Indians Fought Back on High Seas." *Times of India* blog, November 4, 2015. timesofindia.indiatimes.com/blogs/tracking-indian-communities/how-indians-fought-back-on-high-seas/.

Naveed, Fahad. "Train to Balochistan." *Herald*, October 8, 2016. herald.dawn.com/news/1153377.

New York Times. "The Empress of India Sold." December 20, 1914. timesmachine.nytimes.com/timesmachine/1914/12/20/301761302.pdf.

Pande, Rekha. "Women in the Hyderabad State in the 19th and 20th Centuries." *Journal of History and Social Sciences* 3, no. 1 (January–June 2012).

Paracha, Nadeem F. "Karachi: The Past Is Another City." *Dawn*, August 25, 2011. dawn.com/news/654449/karachi-the-past-is-another-city.

Parihar, Subash, "Riddle of Anarkali and Her Tomb." *Tribune*, April 8, 2000. m.tribuneindia.com/2000/20000408/windows/main5.htm.

Pathak, Sushmita. "The Rocky Road to Saving Hyderabad's Stunning Geology." Atlas Obscura, April 22, 2022. atlasobscura.com/articles/hyderabad-rocks.

Porecha, Maitri. "When the Indian Railways Stumbled upon 19th Century Documents That Revealed Its Lost Rail Line in Pakistan." *Hindu*, April 25, 2023. thehindu.com/society/april-16-rail-day-indian-railways-19th-century-documents-show-bolan-pass-rail-line-partition-pakistan/article66723820.ece.

Punjab Archives and Libraries. "Tomb of Anarkali." alw.punjab.gov.pk/anarkali-tomb.

Puroshotham, Sunil. "Internal Violence: The 'Police Action' in Hyderabad." *Comparative Studies in Society and History* 57, no. 2 (April 2015): 435–66. jstor.org/stable/43908352.

Rachini, Mouhamad. "100 Job Applications Later, This Newcomer Still Can't Restart His Engineering Career in Canada." *The Current*, CBC Radio, November 10, 2023. cbc.ca/radio/thecurrent/b-c-legislation-migrant-employment-barriers-1.7021432.

Rahman, M. "Indian Shipping Pioneer Scindia Steam in Serious Trouble." *India Today*, July 31, 1987. indiatoday.in/magazine/economy/story/19870731-indian-shipping-pioneer-scindia-steam-in-serious-trouble-799109-1987-07-30.

Ray, Sanjana. "This Nizam Used a Rs 1000 Cr Diamond as Paperweight, Owned 50 Rolls-Royce Cars & Had Rs 19 Lakh Crore of Net Worth." *GQ India*, January 22, 2023. gqindia.com/get-smart/content/nizam-used-rs-1000-cr-diamond-as-paperweight-50-rolls-royce-cars-rs-19-lakh-crore-net-worth.

Reinhardt, Anne. "Shipping Nationalism in India and China, 1920–52." In *Beyond Pan-Asianism: Connecting China and India, 1840s–1960s*, edited by Tansen Sen and Brian Tsui, 378–409. Delhi: Oxford University Press. doi.org/10.1093/oso/9780190129118.003.0014.

Royal Museums Greenwich. House Flag, Scindia Steam Navigation Co. Ltd. rmg.co.uk/collections/objects/rmgc-object-357.

Sayeed, Vikhar Ahmed. "Hyderabad's Dark History: A Tale of Two Massacres." Frontline, November 10, 2023. frontline.thehindu.com/the-nation/history-a-tale-of-two-massacres-in-hyderabad-karnataka-razakars-1948-police-action-annexation-of-hyderabad-nizam-anti-muslim-attacks-kalaburagi-bidar/article67442047.ece.

Singha, Radhika. "The Great War and a 'Proper' Passport for the Colony: Border-Crossing in British India, c.1882–1922." *Indian Economic and Social History Review* 50, no. 3 (2013): 289–315. warwick.ac.uk/fac/arts/history/ghcc/event/profrsinghaiasfellow/indian_economic_social_history_review-2013-singha-289-3151.pdf.

Tharoor, Shashi. 2017. "'But What about the Railways …?' The Myth of Britain's Gifts to India." *Guardian*, November 25, 2017. theguardian.com/world/2017/mar/08/india-britain-empire-railways-myths-gifts.

Tharoor, Shashi. *Inglorious Empire: What the British Did to India.* London: Hurst, 2016.

The Indian Listener, July 31, 1947. (Program journal of All India Radio, New Delhi.)

Thompson, Mike. "Hyderabad 1948: India's Hidden Massacre." BBC News, September 24, 2013. bbc.co.uk/news/magazine-24159594.

Time. "Hyderabad: Silver Jubilee Durbar." February 22, 1937. content .time.com/time/subscriber/article/0,33009,770599,00.html.

United Nations. Department of International Economic and Social Affairs. "Population Growth and Policies in Mega Cities." Policy paper no. 13, ST/ESA/SER.R/77 (1988). population.un.org/wup/Archive/ Files/1988_Karachi.PDF.

Vaidya, Tridiv. "Kutchis Dream about Steamer Service to Karachi." *Times of India,* January 6, 2004. timesofindia.indiatimes.com/city/ ahmedabad/kutchis-dream-about-steamer-service-to-karachi/ articleshow/408503.cms?utm_source=contentofinterest&utm_ medium=text&utm_campaign=cppst.

Wire. "Will the Government Finally Take a Decision about Mumbai's Jinnah House?" April 4, 2017. thewire.in/politics/will-government- finally-take-decision-mumbais-jinnah-house.

Zamindar, Vazira. *The Long Partition and the Making of Modern South Asia: Refugees, Boundaries, Histories.* New York: Columbia University Press, 2007.

© Lisa Vlasenko

SADIYA ANSARI is a Pakistani Canadian journalist based in London, England. Her work has appeared in the *Guardian*, *VICE*, *Refinery29*, *Maclean's*, *The Walrus*, and the *Globe and Mail*, among others. She has reported from North America, Asia, and Europe, and her work has changed legislation and won awards. She is co-founder of the group Canadian Journalists of Colour, a 2021 R. James Travers Foreign Corresponding Fellow, and a 2023–24 Asper Visiting Professor at the University of British Columbia.